THE PARTNERS WITHIN

The Partners Within

Personal Growth
and
Global Spirituality

ROBERT C. FELIX

The Partners Within
Personal Growth and Global Spirituality

www.partnerswithin.com
www.global-spirituality.com
Cover design by jackhiller.com

This book is dedicated to my son Joel,
An accomplished wordsmith in his own right,
And an invaluable contributor to this book.

And

Tony, Howard, Madeline, and Mary

CONTENTS

INTRODUCTION

The Place of the Spiritual

Once, people believed that they existed in a world closely connected to the Divine. When individuals, whether they were kings, queens, shamans or shepherds, were confused by a dilemma, a god would appear and speak to them. Our literature is one long testament to this connection between gods and man; from Homer's *Iliad* to Judaism's *Torah*, down to St. Paul on the road to Damascus, the historical record of humanity is one long conversation between the human and the Divine.

Today, however, few of us feel strongly connected to a power greater than our own. Our modern world races ahead with high technology, space flights, complex issues with international governments, and the fierce competition that exists between all citizens to prosper. No wonder many people today read the stories of that earlier age as fables. Although most of us continue to believe in some form of God/Divine, many of us consider the prospect of contact with this higher source as the delusion of some private individuals' wish.

But it is a sad mistake to believe that people are alone in the universe. We begin to consider the duality of human and divine with a hypothetical question: Who will listen to you when you need advice or help? And, does God listen to us when we pray?

Behind each question is a fundamental issue, one as old as humanity itself: the question of whether we are alone in the universe. In order to get to the spiritual side of this question, we need to look beyond the immediate surroundings of family, friends, community, etc. This question has taken many forms over the years and in contemporary times has become a question about starships and aliens. In this we see how the modern, secular imagination still feels a need to imagine a distant, possibly compassionate presence of a power greater than man. It seems that one defining condition of all of human life is the need to feel for a presence beyond the reality that our senses perceive: the spiritual.

But the spiritual world has never been so challenged by the philosophies of "reality" as it is today. In order to recover the ground between you and the Divine, you must first ask yourself, unequivocally, what it is that you feel inside of yourself when you ask the question, "Am I alone?"

The Role of Institutions

The vast majority of people, everywhere in the world, are raised to believe in some form of God. Therefore, the most common answer to the question of "Am I alone?" is a resounding "No!" This is usually brought about by a faith-based belief system taught by their family, clan or church. For many of us, however, the God of the churches is an impersonal god; a deity closely guarded by the doctrine of the religious institutions. That is where the question "Am I alone?" becomes more challenging. If we feel that God is theirs and not ours, we may feel cut off from the power of God. For the people who may still believe in God but are not so sure about their inherited religion, they may give an answer to this question as "sometimes." This is a typical response in America today: We continue to believe in God, but are skeptical that God listens to every one of us, individually. Finally, others will forcefully reject all institutional teaching and simply accept the human reality around them.

What is clear in the range of answers to the question "Am I alone?" is that there is no single answer. And in a democratic, free and global society this fact rings more clearly each day. Within the global village that exists in almost any American town, there is, no doubt, a wide range of divergent belief systems: Christian, Islamic, Judaic, Gnostic, Hindu, Buddhist, and more. Even among the devoutly affiliated, you would be hard pressed to find people side by side in the same pew who would answer the question, "Am I alone?" exactly the same.

It is one of the great tragedies of our day that so few of us feel connected to a power greater than our own—a power greater than our human will of self-determination. Indeed, in the everyday world of modern life it is hard to feel the presence of the Divine. Many philosophers, scholars and poets have speculated on the lack of presence of God in modern life. Some have suggested that science killed God, or that modern politics separated Church and State, thus diminishing God's role in civic life. Others feel that modern technology has separated people from the rural, agrarian lives where people felt that God provided for their needs with a bountiful harvest. Clearly, in contemporary times, maintaining "the faith" has evolved from being an obligation to being a choice.

While belief in a God, or godliness, is held by nearly all of humanity all across the globe, the interpretation of daily reality and the acceptance of belief systems are matters that individuals decide for themselves. You could be told from the age of two that God is watching you and sitting in judgment, but odds are you will come to your own conclusions about God and whether God is listening.

What we see from these scenarios is that the relationship between the world and the God/Divine is one of people's most personal beliefs. And, as there is a wide variety in the degree of acceptance of faith-based belief systems, how this question is answered is often fundamental to almost everything that people do in life. It is reflected in how they act, how they think, what they want from life and love, and what they believe. The result is that people appear to live in different worlds from each other when they make decisions based on their "faith." Little wonder that real world outcomes range from nations invading nations to clerics advocating terror and murder in order to further goals. Why is this?

There is no single answer to this question, of course, because each person defines their reality. Everybody needs to negotiate their boundaries between religious instruction and personal significance. But many of us with a traditional Western background have, I find, simply stopped praying. Why? Because many have lost a sense that we are truly talking to God through the repetition of standard acts of prayer. The problem is that it is too easy to become absorbed in only the talking of the prayer—or to be limited to the words of ancient traditions—obscuring the ability to listen. For many of us, our mantras have evolved form "Give us this day our daily bread…" to "If it is going to be, it is up to me."

So why must our idea of God be so ancient? In the above examples, God is an old-fashioned idea, a symbol of a "belief" at best. Perhaps the problem is that our notion of this Divine is so ancient. Indeed, many modern believers would scoff at any claim for the name of a godliness that did not actually physically manifest as a person in the period costume of Ancient Judea. And there are some who will remain steadfastly determined that when Jesus returns to Earth, he will be returning to save the true believers alone.

Though the age of miracles seems to have been put on hold, we should not forget that the message of Jesus was one of liberation: "I say unto you ask, and it shall be given you; seek and you will find. Knock and it will be opened for you." (Matthew 7, 7). Or consider: "Listen to me! You can pray for anything and, if you believe, you can have it, it's yours!" (Mark 12, 22-4). Jesus called for you to liberate your mind by seeing the "God within," the holiness of God made within you. To accept the message of Jesus is to see the Christ within you, to see the Divine possibilities of your own life.

Talk and Listen

But unfortunately, the messages of many of the Christian churches, as well as the messages seen in other mainstream orthodox practices, endlessly articulate how to *believe* in God while spending little or no time in developing a method for you to *listen* to God. So because you are a unique individual, with a unique personality, no one can create in you an ability to hear God but you. Therefore, everyone needs to communicate with their own "God/Divine" within themselves. In order to believe that we are "not alone," each of us has to feel the presence of God. This is easy to do when you choose to believe that God is love—and only love—pure and simple. Then you simply let this Spirit of Love help you with making decisions, affecting you in profound, life-changing ways.

Most of the churches of today continue to maintain an excellent job of upholding the moral code and they are unrivaled in their traditional roles of sanctifying life's passages. They also offer a wonderful sense of community for like-minded believers and they do an excellent job of celebrating holidays, holy days and the Sabbath. Obviously, these practices offer a core competency for the social side of human nature. If you are already attending or adhering to the faiths of one of the classic religious traditions, and there is the message of love, there should be no need to change your commitments. The ideas offered here should only be complimentary to your practices, not an alternative.

The Philosophy

The philosophy of The Partners Within creates the grounds to link the concept of the *"me,"* to the *"you,"* and most importantly, to the *"we,"* or all of humanity. The idea of humanity itself is an evolving concept. Throughout prehistory, our sense of the whole of our species was defined by allegiances that were initially limited to families, clans and religions. In more recent centuries, we have included corporations, cities, regions and nation-states. Today we need to re-cast the image of humanity in order to stabilize the human race's relationship to its only home, the planet Earth. With a global population destined to multiply to nearly ten billion by 2050, humanity is about to reach limits to the amount of energy and natural resources that can be consumed. The ongoing global economic boom is creating an exponential demand for decent land, air, water and energy that will some-day overwhelm supply. How we deal with these coming crises will require a global awareness of what is right for all of Earth's life. Like it or not, we are all global citizens. But what is sadly lacking today is a global acceptance of the fact that we are all equally responsible and that we all need to be equally involved. The success of our planet's future depends on it.

In the United States we see this in the narrow-minded pursuit of competitive advantage over other nations that compelled George Bush II to reject the Kyoto protocols. But the United States isn't the only nation that is pursuing industrial growth with little to no admission that everyone on planet Earth needs to breathe the same air. Politicians, bureaucrats, corporations and everyday people need not let the complexities of international accords stop them from this necessary recognition. This book uses pure love, an absolute love that simply wants what is best for all. The very salvation and prosperity of the human race depends on it.

The solutions for this global spirituality start with the premise that the vast majority of people everywhere believe in some form of a "higher power" that created and maintains the mysterious universe that supports us all. From ancient cave paintings to Egyptian pyramids, the prehistoric records are filled with artifacts that represent humanity's reverence of a power higher than its own. More recent studies support this premise. One study located a potential "god gene": a genetic sequence that occurs in nearly all individuals who identified themselves as believing in a "God." Also, public opinion polls taken over the past half century consistently show around ninety-five percent of the world's population believing in a power greater than the human race. But just because people believe in a higher power doesn't mean they use it.

To believe in a higher power is the first step; feeling a connection to that power is far more difficult. Complicating mankind's journey is the fact that the world has so many diverse versions of "God." In fact, only about one half of the world's population believes in the Western definition of God. Contrast this with the Eastern hemisphere's beliefs that include multiple varieties of the Divine. Here, we see many regional variations such as Brahman, Nirvana, Dao, the Great Spirit, and others. Therefore, in this book, we are using the contraction of "God/Divine" to represent the global tradition of god.

We continue to see many avenues of spiritual energy that assist people in their pursuit of love, peace and enlightenment. Most of the Western belief-systems evolved alongside the evolution of monotheism: the belief that there is only one God. But just because writing began to catch on a couple of thousand years ago doesn't mean that the myths of those earlier times are any more relevant than the myths of today. Further, I would argue that the very basis of monotheism may be in conflict with our global reality, as it depends on the rejection of all other forms of the Divine. The legacy of Abraham, Jesus and Mohammed taught us that God is love, and that our role is to love and trust God. This love is open to all but the love of life need not be limited to God. It also needs to be a love for ourselves; the other people involved in our lives, as well as for the intricate web of life that supports us all.

In addition, we need to be aware of the many pros and cons of human nature. The philosophy here helps us see that, although each of us has an infinite variety of strength and weaknesses that we all need to deal with, we also have free will and therefore what we do with our lives is entirely up to us. And because we are socially dependent on others by nature, we naturally want to get along with one another. This means that the vast majority of us want to "do the right thing." Unfortunately, we don't always know how.

Further complicating human nature is the differences between thinking about problems and learning how to solve them. When someone is asked to "think about" something, the response is usually to consider what they have learned in their past. This is easy to do, but the more challenging task is to learn a new way of thinking in regards to an idea or problem. We are generally slower to "learn" something new, particularly as we age.

Another limitation is the human predisposition that limits its loving potential to whatever it finds lovable. People are quick to turn negative toward anything that they don't understand or that they find offensive. And most of us do not like uncertainties and mysteries. We have a tendency to provide answers, regardless of whether they are right or wrong, and are reluctant to admit when we really "don't know." Finally, social scientists have shown that, on average, humans are pretty good at knowing and trusting up to about one hundred and fifty people in their social lives. When we get involved with groups much beyond this size, particularly with people on the other side of the world, it is easy to simply dismiss them as "strangers."

Pure love addresses all of these considerations. It suggests that we need to learn a new awareness of our three major choices in life: 1) what is right for ourselves, 2) what is right for the other people involved in our lives, and 3) what is right for the rest of this world. Almost all of us almost always want to do the right thing for ourselves and the other people we know, but dealing with the rest of humanity is far more complicated. The Partners Within is designed to help us learn what is right for all three of these potentially harmonious yet frequently conflicting choices, the differences between the "me," the "you," and the "we."

So in order to build common ground toward a global belief system, one that works toward all people working toward global responsibility and spirituality, I propose a new universal understanding of the God/Divine. Unlike the rigid dogmas that underlie faith-based belief systems, this book suggests that individuals use the *unconditional* love that exists everywhere in the world's traditions. Without it, our species will find it increasingly difficult to prosper.

Just as we are concerned about finding the proper balance between ourselves and the other people in our lives, we need to be as concerned about our proper balance with the rest of the world. I propose here, and throughout this book, in using "Pure Love," and the "Spirit of Love" as descriptions of this unconditional love. It is a love so pure, it shows us the way to learn right from wrong, good from bad, love from fear, and trust from doubt. After all, we are but a single species sharing a single planet and we are all dependent on one another for our very survival and success.

And where might this pure love come from? From a factual standpoint, nobody really knows. It could come from inside of ourselves as we all have the abilities for both personal and unconditional love. Or it could come from the people that surround us. Social evidence suggests that the benevolence of decent people everywhere can be contagious, resulting in the collective goodwill of humanity extending circles of trust. Or it could come from some larger mystical force that is more powerful than anything the human race is capable of, maybe the God/Divine or, more gloriously, the Spirit of Love. Readers should feel free to decide what works best for them. Personally, I recommend "covering all bases" by believing in all three possibilities.

The powers of Pure Love—and its companion of Pure Light—are so great that they only want what is right for you, the people involved in your life, as well as all of humanity. They enable us to see and act in ways that were too obscure to have been seen before. They inspire us to heal the many diverse challenges of human life, resulting in a better global awareness of our environment. They transform an "us versus them" mentality to a belief-system that respects the fact that "we are all in this together." And ultimately, they offer a conviction that each and every one of us is responsible for what belongs to us all: our only home, the Planet Earth. The salvation of the human race depends on it.

So how do we bring more pure love into our lives? This book uses partnerships between Western style introspection and classic Eastern meditation. These partnerships employ the universally accepted theory of brain specialties by bringing together your "thinking/talking" skills with your "listening/learning" skills. By partnering these two skills together with the Spirit of love, you develop a whole-brain basis that forges a channel to wisdom far greater than your regular conscious thoughts.

This is all it takes to bring yourself into a state of harmony with your world and thus you begin to hear the answers that your spiritual powers have to offer. They light your way and answer you back. They energize your life by inspiring compassion and respect. This is achieved by opening up to the most cherished partnerships of all: the partnerships between you, Pure Love, and all of Earth's life.

Part I of this book focuses on introspection and its uses for acquiring the self-understanding so vital for personal growth and global awareness. It details the major dualistic challenges of human nature and many readers may want to start looking into this aspect right away. Others may want to read through to Part II, which concentrates on meditation. But first, I would recommend mastering the use of introspection in order to gain a better understanding of who you are and what you are doing with your life. Then, by using pure love as the energy for balancing your dualities, it guides you to a new understanding and appreciation for yourself and the rest of your world.

Part II offers a more in depth explanation of meditation and its relationship to global spirituality It starts with the power of a duality between your brain and mind that, coupled with the self-imagination of three-word meditations, leads to a better understanding and use of the four functions of the infamous body, mind, heart and soul.

Part III of this book, "Perspectives," supports the basic message that you can help yourself to be a healthier, more loving and creative individual. This growth is needed throughout our planet but it has to come to us one by one. Ultimately, we will find comfort and security in the realization that we are but a single species sharing a single planet and that we are all in this life together. And by using the evolutionary and loving techniques of your partners within, together, we can make this a better world for all.

As we bring more love into our lives, we magnify our sense of feeling loved. We expand the excitement and joy of being truly alive. We become empowered to love and act in the spirit of good will for ourselves and for all of Earth's life. The God/Divine is still with us and touches our everyday lives. In the words of 14th century Florentine poet Dante Alighieri, "God is the love that moves the sun and all the stars." We need only to seek it and listen.

PART I

PERSONAL GROWTH

INTROSPECTION

In a series of stunning breakthroughs, 21ST century medical science has found in a number of studies that introspection and meditation can transform negative habits and thought patterns into positive energy and emotions. State-of-the-art research labs are using supercharged electroencephalograph (EEG) machines that peer deep into the brain and show the changing electrical patterns of different brain activities. Functional Magnetic Resonance Imaging (fMRI) machines pinpoint the active regions of the brain to within a millimeter, thereby allowing more accurate assessments of the brain's innermost workings. Positron Emission Tomography (PET scans) machines detect regional blood flow in the brain in order to further differentiate between what researchers call the "structural" aspects of the "brain" and the "functioning" aspects of the "mind."

Thanks to these advancements, scientists are able to better define the dualistic aspects of the human experience. As a result, they have determined that even though the mind is different than the brain, they are just like the rest of the human body; *and they can both be intentionally improved for the better.* Now, with these new studies, scientists can join with us whose faith and culture has already confirmed the spirit of love.

Introspection and meditation are the tools for unlocking that love. Using introspection helps you to a better understanding of the duality of your "head" and your "heart." Meditation is used to further define the differences that arise between yourself and the other people involved in your life. When used in sequence, introspection and meditation are especially useful in improving your most basic inherited and learned mental habits.

Western science, beholden to its methodologies of evidence and proof, may be beginning to understand what humanity has always known to be true: there is always a better way. But neither the scientists nor countless faith-based belief systems have focused on one of the most crucial aspects of combining the "talking" of introspection with the "listening" of meditation: uniting these dual energies by allowing unconditional love in your life. This three-way approach helps you overcome negative behavior by releasing the positive dynamics of personal partnerships between the structural features of your brain and the functioning aspects of your mind. They enable you to create a better understanding of yourself, the other people involved in your life, as well as a spiritual awareness of all of Earth's life.

These partnerships start with the two separate yet equal forces of human nature most commonly recognized as dualities: the distinction between intellect and emotions is but one. These dual aspects are also experienced as the differences that sometimes arise between your analytical and intuitive skills, your personal and social lives, your personal growth and global spirituality. By better understanding the strengths and weaknesses of all of your dualistic partnerships, you will gain new insights and perspectives on the differences between the possibly conflicting yet potentially harmonious opposites of your personality.

The goal is to help you nurture the highest spiritual powers that you are capable of. This is where you discover a "third way": a path to the Spirit of Love, the highest level of consciousness. This path does not mistake narrow selfishness or wishful fantasies as goals. Instead, it is a connected consciousness that enables you to unite the self-interest human powers that want what is best for you; the selfless higher powers that want what is best for the other people in your life; and the collective highest powers that want what is best for all. This series of steps can be described as a Human—Higher—Highest trinity, where the 'highest' results in a greater good. This is the foundation of all of the partners within. They rely on the power of words to assist you in moving from one level of good to the next higher level as you relate to your understanding of yourself, the other people in your life, and the rest of the world.

Some dualities are frequently personal concerns—most people use their intellect to act professionally in the workplace, while using their loving emotions to nurture their family. But some of our other dualities, such as the ones between our past and our present life, or between ourselves and others, can be a source of more public concern. These may result in unbalanced decisions, frustrations, or sometimes even outright conflict. Think about how often people's differences collapse into the struggles of the "me versus you" or the "us versus them." Or consider the conflicts that frequently arise from unbalanced decisions that depend on fundamentalism rather than liberalism and do not consider the best of interests of both. Worse yet are the tragedies of "local versus global," or increasingly, "the economy versus the environment." In these examples, we see people's personal preferences and beliefs affecting their choices—and an almost total lack of wanting what is best for all.

Balancing Dualities through Partnerships

How often do you find yourself facing a choice between the intellect of your 'head' and the emotions of your 'heart?' Or how about the choices that sometimes arise between your thoughts and feelings, your past and the present you face, or between your reality and your ideals? Probably not very often and that can be a problem. In order to learn how to make better choices for living your life to the fullest, you need to learn how to pay attention to who you are and what you are doing with your life. This book starts with an easy technique for understanding yourself by showing you how to make more balanced decisions through the use of introspection. When this form of self-knowledge is coupled with pure love and light, it is particularly adept at helping us to stay on top of the dualistic challenges of everyday life.

Unfortunately, modern life drives many of us to a level of activity and stress where we wind up using predetermined choices for many of our daily challenges. We may "think about" what we are doing based on our memories and beliefs but "learning" from our experiences becomes an exception, particularly as we age. After all, life is complicated enough as is and there are many times when it is simply easier to use our faith and beliefs (our most basic, unreflective assumptions) for making decisions, regardless of how poorly they work or how inappropriate they may be.

Some common examples of predetermined choices are often found in the everyday duality of science and faith. Science uses the generally accepted principles of the scientific method in order to help us with understanding our world and the way it works. Faith gives us answers to the unanswerable as there are always some phenomena that cannot be explained. Even though the most basic duality of "truth in science" and "belief in faith" may be in direct opposition to each other, most of us find a happy medium that allows this duality to be peacefully balanced within ourselves. However, there are often a few unbalanced individuals who lose sight of this potentially agreeable duality and simply throw logic out the window and rely solely on the "blind" emotions of their faith. As a worst-case example, the results can be martyrdom, terror and murder. Fortunately, the pen is mightier than the sword.

A duality, then, is a pair of forces that are opposites of each other. In our everyday Western culture, these dualities are most commonly recognized as the divide between your head and heart. In the Eastern culture, they are known as the "yin" and "yang," or the potentially harmonious interplay of the opposites of the universe.

Indeed, dualities can be as broad as the distinction between life and love. The goal is to make these one and the same but far too often they lead us to emphasize one at the expense of the other. The dualistic introspections offered in this book give you the opportunity to think about the times when you might be of "two minds" about some of the more common dilemmas you encounter in your daily life. This book uses pure and universal love to bridge these gaps.

Pure love helps us find solutions to our everyday concerns and goals. It is an unconditional love, a love so pure that it creates love when none exists. It not only helps us with what is right for our personal challenges but it also helps us with what is right for the other people in our life, and eventually, it helps us toward a better understanding of the mother Earth that supports us all. Human beings are certainly *capable* of Pure Love—Buddha, Jesus, Mohammad and Gandhi were excellent examples—but, for most of us, it does not come easily. Indeed, human love is usually limited to what it finds lovable and at best is indifferent to everything else. At its worst, human emotions can turn negative or even destructive toward anything they find unlikable or unpleasant. The spirit of love simply wants what is best for all.

This technique starts by forming partnerships between our talking and listening abilities. We use our *talking* skills in the form of introspection. We then use our *listening* skills in the form of meditation. These partners also represent the coming together of the two separate yet equal forces of *thinking* and *learning*. Just because we think about our concerns and goals doesn't necessarily mean we learn about them. These partnerships will be unique to you, as you and your personal spiritual powers are the only ones who could possibly understand your unique journey. They will assist you with structuring your life so that you can function at your best. They can be used for personal growth, physical and emotional health, global awareness and the greater good.

In the global reality of the 21st century, the time is ripe for combining these dualities in order to create new, more effective practices. The partners within techniques offer an easy method by showing you how to bring the best of introspection together with the best of meditation. When your thoughts enter into the realm of introspection, you stimulate your ability to analyze the difference between right and wrong, good and bad. When your feelings enter into the subtle universe of meditation, you inspire your ability to intuit the difference between love and fear, trust and doubt. And whenever introspection and meditation are partnered together through the use of pure love, a balanced "partnership of equals" is built between your personal dualistic abilities and your ever-expanding global awareness. This is how you learn what is best for yourself, others and for all of Earth's life. Because whenever your dualities work together for the benefit of each other, you will have found a pathway to the highest spiritual energies of the universe, the fountainhead of Pure Love and Light. Introspection is for understanding your concerns. Meditation is for achieving your goals. Obviously, *we need to do both.*

From mainstream psychology to the cutting edge of empowerment theory, this dualistic theory of reality has now been widely accepted. When opposing forces stop competing for self-gratification, and agree to support and enable each other, then these partnerships will begin releasing your higher possibilities. They help you to make your decisions more balanced and your motives wiser. The results will be the growth of more harmonious, mutually supportive skills. Now let us look a little more closely at how the partnerships between introspection and meditation actually work.

Introspection/Meditation

The Partners Within uses a dual process. In the first step, a memorable paring of words is used to stimulate introspection into situations that present you with possible conflicts. By voicing these words you are able to identify the potential conflict between the choices you make and how you respond to your many diverse challenges. You gain insight into how some of the contrasting aspects of your personality might be competing with each other or, more frequently, how one may be dominating the other, resulting in unbalanced decisions. Structured introspection activates the active-talking side of your personality that expresses the voice of your innermost concerns and goals. It allows you to gain insight into how you are influenced by the potentially conflicting aspects of your personality.

In the second step, the third word of each partner within is used as a guide to the spiritual resolutions of pure light and love that are available from the introspections and meditations used throughout this book. You achieve this passive-listening state by using the colors, chakras and a pure white light. This is where you will find the spiritual resolutions for the pros, cons, compromises and solutions that affect your most personal concerns. The results are the answers that help you analyze problems, prioritize goals and assist you in going forward with your life.

Introspection

Introspection has long been associated with the psychoanalytic traditions developed in the Western hemisphere of the world. It is the thoughtful and reflective sides of human nature and its goal is to examine all of your behaviors, thoughts, feelings and beliefs in order to determine how they affect your life, for better or worse. Here, the structure of introspection is guided by using the contrasting aspects of human nature known as dualities. It is a process that helps you uncover the unique way in which you look at the world and how you make sense of it. It uses your logical-verbal skills to foster greater communication and insight into your unique personality.

In introspection, you will want to let the conversations and feelings flow freely between all aspects of your personality. This is where you will explore the different features of your dualistic nature through the use of reflection, contemplation and mindfulness. Where you might commonly find concern at this stage is in the discovery of how your perceptions of the present may differ with the experiences of your past. Other times you will uncover the different motives behind your intellect and your emotions. Frequently, conflicts arise from an imbalance between your wants and needs. Sometimes it is not uncommon to find disturbances between yourself and the other people that are involved in your life. After you have discovered sources of concern or conflicting goals, *do not judge*, just accept the differences as part of your journey through life. In this first step of introspection, the objective is to define your concerns and goals. Then you will be ready for the next step: seeking the solutions of pure love through the use of meditation.

Introspection (or what could be considered meditation "lite") is a simple form of seeking insight that can be practiced in as little as a few minutes a day. It is designed for the average person who has a busy life. This method works for those of us that have not been trained from childhood on meditation practices. It relies on skills for talking, rather than listening, which suits our more extroverted environment. This introspection is structured to provide personal insight to those of us attuned to the global-consciousness and its most common rewards and failures. It is designed to open up our awareness and define our ideals. It is the form of meditation that is best used to attend to the daily maintenance of the self. It works best when you can achieve a state of mind that allows you to pay close attention to a topic. It does not work as well when you are stressed or engaged in heavy physical activity. Here, it is known as the *"alpha"* waves of the brain that are characterized by whenever you are awake and relaxed. It can be practiced virtually anytime when you have a few free minutes. All you need to do is relax and take a few deep breaths. Then you can either close your eyes or simply stare off into some stationary space. A further description of the introspection process will be found in the rest of Part I of this book.

Meditation

Meditation, which is explored in more detail in Part II, evolved in the Eastern hemisphere of our globe. This deeper, more intense form of insight arose from the need to become quiet and to listen to the more subtle energies of your brain-mind partnerships (or possibly the universe) in order to receive enlightenment. It was thought that this listening might show a path to the higher powers of compassion and respect and for thousands of years the practice has brought countless generations to this holistic-creative aspect of human nature. Eastern meditation techniques stem from many sources across the Asian continent, and entire religions have been founded on subtle differences of meditation goals and practices. Mindfulness, transcendental, yoga, tai chi, and zen are but a few examples. Most use the broad based *"gamma"* waves of the brain and there is an overall emphasis on excluding the mental-verbal "voice" from meditation, i.e., the inner monologues by which we "hear ourselves" think. The limitation of this method for many Westerners is that few have the time to train themselves to meditate with the deep intensity that many Easterners, trained from birth, are able to achieve. But the popularity of many gurus and Eastern-inspired masters testifies to the Western public's thirst for the personal growth knowledge that seems to be within the grasp of meditation.

Global Awareness

It took a trip to the moon for humanity to see, in one photograph, the stark reality that the Earth is truly unique, and that all the people on that earth have one shared destiny. In 1968, as US astronauts circled the moon in advance of a planned lunar landing, one photograph captured the earth in a photo that has shaken many from the dogged belief that the actions and fortunes of "strangers" is not a personal concern. The photo, later dubbed "Earthrise" by the press, shows the Earth half lit by the sun hovering in the hostile vacuum of space. It was influential on the budding "whole earth" movements of the 1960's and 1970's, a spirit that lives on with the "green" movements of today. The 21st Century climate awareness and energy concerns are a continuation of these traditions.

The goal of The Partners Within is to liberate us toward a global recognition and understanding that we are all undeniably involved in this world together. As more and more people are included in the global economy, the truth of that picture continues to unfold before us all today. The human race in its entirety has to develop a deeper commitment to the collective picture of who we are and what we are doing to our only home, the planet Earth. A huge transformation is needed in our realization that we are all involved in this together. Otherwise, some time this century, we will literally burn up our livelihoods and condemn billions to extinction. The solution is simple. We need to realize that we are as dependent upon other people as they are dependent upon us. Then, by following the partner within sequence of "left-right-whole," we will grow our ability to include all people into the all-inclusive "you, me and we." This is facilitated when everyone energizes their personal and universal powers of pure and unconditional love.

Getting Started

In getting started with introspection, you first need to put your world on pause, find a place where you can relax and won't be disturbed. Become totally quiet. No matter what your specific focus is that day, it helps to start with a few chants of the partner within of "Life—Love—Light" (detailed at the end of Part I). Relax your body and mind by taking several deep breaths. The "Life" is your left-brain's reality and intellect; your desire to do the right thing. The "Love" is your right-brain's emotions and spirit; your desire to do well for the other people involved in your life. The "Light" is your whole-brain's desire for global spirituality, and then the next step, global citizenship.

The assumption here is that pure life, love and light come from the same source. But, as you know, when light is fractured through a prism, it results in a rainbow of seven colors. It follows, then, that pure love is contained in each of the pure colors along with its own unique insights and characteristics. These seven colors are then partnered with a modernized version of the ancient Hindu Chakras, the seven metaphysical energy centers of the human body. Along with each chakra, there is also a warning about seven pairs of deadly sins. These sins could be a result of either a malfunction or disease in the chakra energy areas.

After a few moments of relaxing, turn to one of the dualities that are outlined in the following ten chapters. Keep in mind, these dualities represent complex issues and it is usually best for beginners to limit themselves to one of them at a time. Think about how they may apply to you and how they may affect your choices in life. Use your verbal and visual skills to further define their unique characteristics. Then it is time to be quiet and meditate on the spirituality implied by the third word. Give yourself a few minutes to let the colors' Spirit of Love sink in. With practice, you will find it easy to go back and forth between your verbalizations and visualizations.

These dualities are traditionally regarded as opposing energies, the classic dualities so deeply rooted in spiritual writings, myths and theory. Frequently, they will be similar to the features that have long been attributed to the left and right hemispheres of the human brain and the similarities are intentional. But be advised that the detailed physiology of the brain is far more complex. The main point here is that with all of your dualities, you will be looking at the most common of the contrasting aspects of human nature in order to seek the balanced solutions to your most important concerns and goals. Indeed, you will soon learn how to recognize the dualistic challenges of your brain and your mind and then you will be well on your way to structuring your life so that you function at your best.

Although the partnerships of this book cover the primary areas where you can grow by bringing your major dualities together, a possible list of subtle combinations is endless. For the sake of clarity, this book offers what I have identified as the most useful ones. Readers should feel free to create their own. But always remember to seek the spirit of love by reflecting with a third word, thereby completing the trinity of a three-word practice.

With these exercises, you will soon discover the compromises and solutions that help you resolve your worries and ambitions. Solutions may come in an instant, later in the day, or gradually over a period of time. You will learn how to make the choices necessary for going forward with your life. Once you have settled your more pressing concerns, you can then begin the spiritual quest for your body's instincts, your mind's innovations, your heart's intuitions, and your soul's inspirations. The journey is yours.

BRILLIANT RED
Radiating from the Pelvic Chakra
INTELLECT—EMOTION—ME

R ed is the first color in the spectrum of light. Here, we use it to become fully independent human beings, capable of seeing through the limitations that exist in the sometimes all too repetitive acts of our behavior, thoughts, feelings and beliefs. When we begin by using Brilliant Red—a Pure Light that radiates from the Pelvic Chakra—we begin a journey of looking inside of ourselves, a journey of discovering our personal uniqueness and autonomy. This pure red light shows us the way to recognize ourselves as unique people that inevitably strive for the best in their bodies, minds, hearts and souls.

Red is the color that helps us to recognize the conflicts that sometimes arise between our 'head and heart,' or our intellect and emotions. Whenever we seek better awareness of these dualistic aspects, we are blending together the powers of our logic and compassion, determination and creativity, reality and intuition, and understanding and respect. By seeking resolution between these typically contrasting aspects of human nature, we begin to reveal the potential of our total being, thereby creating better solutions for all.

First, find a spot that you can make your own, a place that is quiet and where you feel comfortable. This may be in your house, a special spot at work, or even outside in a park. This should be your personal ritual place, somewhere you will not be disturbed, and you allow yourself to relax. Let the conflicts between your intellect and emotions come to mind. Do not judge, accept them as they are, and start this introspection session by feeling the love of a Brilliant Red Light helping you to identify and learn about your personal uniqueness.

The Duality of Intellect and Emotion

In your mind's eye, picture the color red and repeat the word "Intellect" until you no longer have the need to speak the word and can think about what intellect means to you. Intellect is the overt, conscious, willful part of your personality that sometimes will be dominant, other times it will be more distant. As you repeat the word 'intellect,' focus on your breath while achieving a place inside yourself where you feel the clarity of a Brilliant Red Light. With this clarity comes a fresh new ability to understand your motivations. What motivates you is usually intellect or emotion, but what you need to see is that conflict between these two is not necessary. Each power will act in its turn as daily life calls forth a response from one or the other. As you think about the word 'intellect' you will see how you can blend your intellect with emotion and your emotion with logic, learning how these dual aspects of your personality can be combined into a more effective being.

Now, while breathing at a slow, steady pace, repeat the word "Emotion." Concentrate on your positive emotions, such as love, kindness, compassion and respect. Ignore any negative emotions that may arise by concentrating on the love that resides in a Brilliant Red Light. The pure red that never leaves this duality is like those valuable mornings where you suddenly wake up with fresh energy and ideas. This energy comes from a mental and spiritual clarity where Red's Spirit of Love is renewing our purpose. It shows us which decisions were made in error from an unbalance of either intellect or emotion. Once you see how easy it is to mistake the one power for the other, you are already on the path to healing any divisions between them. Red, like a new day, is offering you the opportunity to be the best that you can possibly be.

Resolution: Me

Red is only one of the seven colors that open the door to love. Chant the word "Me." This is the unity of intellect and emotion; a total person that allows us to be wise in our passions and passionate in our wisdom. Continue to feel how your intellect and emotions are complimenting and empowering one another. Intellect and emotion, now identified in the various and changing continuum of motivation, are offering new insight into each other. Intellect makes clear the distinction between right and wrong, good and bad. Emotion shows us the differences between love and fear, trust and doubt. Although emotion has little instruction on how to negotiate what is right and wrong, intellect does. But intellect is slow to heal a painful loss or hurt feelings by itself. Now you see how the power of red helps you to grow your total being because it offers a dual reservoir of energy for you to use.

The energy to harmonize intellect and emotion is yours. If you experience regret while using this introspection, then you are uncovering a painful rift between them. Use a few seconds to recognize that division—it is a part of human life—then let it be healed with a Brilliant Red Light. Eventually, your greatest accomplishments will come when your intellect is validated by reality and your emotions are motivated by love. The power of a pure and universal love will only increase in your life, creating an ever-improving "me."

The Functions of Brilliant Red

Red empowers the body's instincts, helping us to identify our unique talents and limitations. For instance, we are all born with a wide variety of strengths and weaknesses. By increasing our awareness of reality, red helps us distinguish between those areas that are under our control and areas over which we have little or no influence.

Red empowers the mind's innovations, creating new solutions for the concerns and goals we face. Within the broad range of intellectual abilities, some of us may have better verbal skills while others may be more mathematically inclined. As we learn to differentiate between our strengths and weaknesses, as well as the strengths and weaknesses of others, red allows us to become more proactive to the circumstances that will benefit from responsible action and less reactive to events beyond our control.

Red empowers the heart's intuitions to better understand ourselves, our family and friends, and our only home, the planet Earth. Red teaches that some of us are born with an emotional nature that is more daring while some are more reserved. As we identify our strengths, we find ways to contribute to the benefit of ourselves and others. When we learn of our vulnerabilities, we know when to seek support.

Red empowers the soul's inspirations to tune into the Pure Love that surrounds us all. A few of us are born with an ample amount of this spiritual power; most of us are still on a journey of discovery and growth. When we open up to the power of brilliant red, we internalize its power, thereby expanding our personal love into a love for all.

Positive and Negative

Recently, Western science has finally confirmed what the wisdom traditions of the Orient have known for millennia: that an introspection/ meditation practice literally and physically improves the functioning aspects of our mind and, in turn, the structure of our brain. Clinical studies have shown that meditation increases the electrical activity in the left prefrontal cortex, an area of the brain that is associated with the positive emotions of love, happiness and joy. It also sends inhibitory signals to the amygdala, an area of the brain that has been shown to be responsible for exacerbating the negative emotions that, if left unrestrained, destroy our personal abilities to grow. These "lower" power emotions can quickly deteriorate into destructive behavior patterns. However, through the use of this partner within, there is no need for anyone to become trapped by negative emotions. We only need to practice our personal powers of pure love. And nobody can do this for us; we have to do it ourselves.

This first stage of personal growth represents our most basic life force, the awareness of our individual identities as well as an awareness of our social needs for safety, procreation and self-improvement. Because this first partnership relates to finding our psychic autonomy while becoming independent human beings, it is reflected in the physical strengths and weaknesses in the foundation of our independence, our pelvic and skeletal system. If you do enjoy good health in these areas, then good balance is indicated. This positive energy is represented by a brilliant red light that radiates freely from the Pelvic Chakra. Blockages in this energy center could be caused by the "deadly sins" of pride and arrogance, leading to problems with becoming caring and productive individuals. Disorders in these areas would indicate that you may want to spend extra time using red's help along with the partnership of Intellect—Emotion—Me.

FIRE ORANGE
Radiating from the Navel Chakra
PAST—PRESENT—FUTURE

O range is the second color in the light spectrum and it corresponds to the second stage of personal growth. This is where we resolve the differences between our past and present, freeing our ability to realistically look at our future. In the first stage we learned how to balance the dualistic energies of our personal self to the larger structure of our total being. Now, we are empowering all of our creative abilities to see the whole potential of human life, with all of its hopes, dreams and goals, mirrored in our vision of the future.

First, we turn to developing our awareness of how the past affects the present and influences our daily choices. The Love of a Fire Orange Light—a Pure Light that radiates from the Navel Chakra—is the energy we use to analyze the memories and emotions of our past so that we can learn from them. This partner's most powerful purpose is to put the painful mistakes of our past—along with the mistakes of others—behind us so we can start to make meaningful progress with our lives. This means forgiveness. Forgiveness, were it easy, would be the most useful of human abilities because it allows us to move forward in life with out hang-ups and resentments. However, forgiveness is one of the more difficult human conditions to arrive at, especially when the aspects of pure self-interest dominate.

Reflect, for a moment, on the personal successes and failures from your past. Think about how they affect the choices you have made and the choices you continue to make. Contrast the reality of your past with the reality of the ever-present "now." Resolve to make decisions that are concerned with what your life is about today. This is where you will free a new vision for your future. As always, the spirit of love that is a Fire Orange Light is available to help.

Orange is the comforting light of the hearth, a light that has lead to restful contemplation in all cultures for countless millennia. How comforting that first firelight must have been, when early man first struggled forth from the fears and vulnerability of the darkness with the taming of the fire!

The Duality of Past and Present

31

The light of Fire Orange has lent itself to contemplation and reflection for millions of years, and now it is the past that we are ready to confront. Repeat the word "Past," keeping a clear picture of a Pure Orange Light. Whatever the first trouble that might pop into your head is, that is where you should focus on forgiveness. Only forgiveness releases negative thoughts and feelings. With your past, whatever you might remember, contains its own solutions. The past is over. It is gone. You cannot fix whatever it is that comes to you as unresolved energies. It needs to be released. Simply seek what is best for all, even in the memories of the things you or other people did that were regretted, turned out wrong, or were simply mistakes.

Now start to repeat the word "Present." Focus your mind by picturing a Fire Orange Light, similar to the light that is given off by the glow of a sparkling fireplace. (How rapidly you want to pace yourself will be determined by what works best for you.) Now the color orange is seeking to relax and comfort you. When you chant the word 'present' softly, reflect on the fact that it is always the ever-present now. The goal is to absorb yourself in the now, to feel that now is the time to learn new perspectives as to who you are and what you are doing with your life. Once you are firmly rooted in the now, Pure Orange will begin to help you to contemplate your future.

Resolution: Future

With the color Orange firmly in mind, begin the chant and your "Future" will be unlocked. The key to your future starts with love for yourself because without self love, it will be impossible to enter into healthy and loving relationships with others. Self love also instructs us in the skills that we are good at. It highlights our strengths and talents, and from these, the services we love to do. By capitalizing on this knowledge, your future awaits. Orange's Spirit of Love enlightens the best of your past along with the best of your present, and then your future will unfold in what is best for both, and from there, what is best for all. Feel the warmth of the color orange beginning a partnership of respect not only between you and the other people involved in your life, but between you and all of the citizens of Earth.

The Functions of Fire Orange

Orange purges the body of doubts while opening up its instinctual awareness of reality. It is used to evaluate the conflicts between your past and your future, helping you to learn what is best in your ever-present now.

Orange empowers the mind to learn from mistakes so that they are avoided in the future. It heals the conflicts between yourself and other people, allowing the innovations of your intellect to guide you in the future.

Orange purifies the heart by cleaning the negative emotions that resulted from relationships that had gone bad, releasing the positive aspects of relationships that promote growth and well-being. Orange nurtures the intuitions that reveal the rewarding aspects of the communities of mankind that are beneficial to all.

Orange opens up the soul's spiritual energy, freeing the creativity of inspiration. Use Orange to give birth to new and better understandings for yourself and others. Orange respects the wisdom that is available from the collective goodwill of humanity, helping to grow global citizenry for all.

Happy and Hurt

This second stage of personal growth is where we liberate the "happy child" within us. Almost everyone has some fond memories from their childhood when they were happy, playful, loving and kind, a time before we became hardened by life. It was a time that was filled with openness, discovery, wonder and love. Our creative, artistic, loving and spiritual abilities still come from reclaiming these passions of our youth. They still exist inside us and can be set free by exploring the partnerships of past, present and future.

However, many of us also have some traumatic memories from our childhood that can be filled with negative emotions. These occur during the inevitable wounding that happens during adolescence and adulthood. Often these memories are buried deep within the brain. They become the "hurt child" that most of us carry around to a greater or lesser degree. These memories can be difficult to verbalize or even remember clearly and then they hinder us in our ability to release their negative hold. Problems may arise when these internal wounds cause negative reactions to similar situations in the present, trapping us in rigid behavior that repeats past responses inappropriately. All memories shape our lives and influence our experiences, learning and goals. If we don't make peace with our past, it will continue to haunt us and hinder our future growth.

This stage of personal growth represents our ability to put the past behind us so that we are open to the positive possibilities that exist in the ever-present now. A Fire Orange Light, radiating from the Navel Chakra, located in the middle of the abdomen, reveals this positive energy. But problems at this stage can be aggravated by frustrations with unresolved issues from the past. They are certainly worsened by the deadly sins of gluttony and intoxication. They may reveal themselves as difficulties with being able to forgive, being sincere and enjoying life. If this occurs, surround the painful memories of the past with the power of a Fire Orange Light and, during the deep intensity of an introspection session, purge them from your body and mind by simply willing them to float out of you and off into the universe. This may take some dedicated effort depending upon the severity of the problem, but the results will be far superior to letting the negativity fester within. Because this second stage of personal growth is so strongly influenced by the frustrations and failures of our past, it has been shown by some that the effectiveness of our digestion and elimination systems can be affected. If physical or psychosomatic problems do arise in these areas, then the use of the Fire Orange Light and the partner within of Past—Present—Future is waiting to help.

GOLDEN YELLOW
Radiating from the Diaphragm Chakra
PERSONAL—SOCIAL—ALL

Yellow is the third stage in personal growth. It is here, along with a Golden Yellow Light, a light that feels similar to a bright kitchen nook on a sunny summer morning, this color brings clarity of focus. In preparing for this introspection session, start your mental pictures by using the most common images of the differences between your personal and social lives that are most important to you. The love of a Golden Yellow Light—radiating from the Diaphragm Chakra—helps us to bridge the differences between ourselves and others by bringing this potentially harmonious duality together for the benefit of all.

One of the most common conflicts we face on a daily basis are the decisions we need to make between doing what is best for ourselves and doing what is best for the other people involved in our lives. Doing what is best for all is still a distant third. Our natural inclination is to think about our personal self-interests. But as social animals, everybody's life is a series of interactions with others and these relationships show us where our larger social responsibilities are. To resolve these dual energies, go inside yourself and acknowledge the pros and cons of any situation where there may be a conflict of goals. Do not judge, simply weigh the relative merits of the different sides of all of the issues, and then become quiet and think about what is best for both. Eventually, you will discover the compromises and solutions that help you to learn what is best for all. And whenever you discover this noble solution, you will receive the greatest reward of all, the growth of your love and passion for being alive.

Whether it is on the level of your own life choices or in matters of public policy, the chain from personal (you) to social (local) to all (global) is based on trust. It is the genesis of our reverence for the diversity and interrelatedness of life, the shining creation of a pure and unconditional love.

The Duality of Personal and Social

Repeat "Personal" while visualizing a Golden Yellow Light. Once you have become comfortable with this introspection, you will find that you can move quickly from the state in which you are merely chanting the words to the absorbed state where the birthplace of new ideas wait. You may find that this visualization easily morphs into an image of a golden yellow sunset or another image of a golden light that inspires your ideal view of nature. Most meditation practices are traditionally focused on removing these images and focusing exclusively on the breathing body and achieving emptiness of the mind. However, if you find that an image works for you, use it. Orthodoxy in any form limits the grandest truth and the unique growth possibilities of each individual. This partnership will help you grow the image of your unique self however you let it.

Once the energy of your personal life has become fully absorbed by the color Yellow, then replace the word with "Social." This is where you expand your awareness of the needs of your local groups: the family, friends, communities, institutions and nations you are involved with. However, you might find that when you are thinking of other people, you may assume that their goals are the same as yours. Personal—Social—All is a corrective to the notion that you must succeed at the cost of others, that you must triumph over others in order to secure your own individuality. Feel your ability to care for the social side of your life growing. During this introspection, look to grow stronger in your love for others; you will only earn more of their love in return. Once you recognize that it is only the Earth's incredible web of life that sustains us, you are ready to contemplate the universal all.

Resolution: All

Now, chant the final stage, the partnered form of this duality, the global "All." This entirety is not only the condition of human existence sprung up out of the void, but is also the conditions that surround the human. It is not simply a vision of one's own being, or even the life of clans or nations, it is a vision of humanity as inseparable from the astronomical fact of the planet itself. When you are contemplating the word 'all,' you will find yourself overcome by a love for creation and for the betterment of all things. This is where you will find the beginning of the desire to merge your interests with others. This is where you will find the balanced solutions that reflect what is best for you, the other people in your life, as well as all of Earth's life. Golden Yellow's Spirit of Love is the guiding light; it increases your spiritual reverence for the incredible Planet Earth. Reflect with yellow on the Earth's abundant resources, its diverse ecosystems, its interrelated life, its fervent growth. The result can only be the growth of the noblest of human aspirations: global awareness, responsibility and citizenship for all.

The Functions of Golden Yellow

Yellow heals the body of distortions of reality. Sometimes people live in a world of fantasy and denial. Yellow assists us in the use of our instinctual abilities, enabling us to correctly interpret our world and see how we best fit into a greater whole.

Yellow cures the mind of illogical thinking. Sometimes people wallow without end in laziness, ignorance and doubt. Yellow stimulates our creativity, enabling our powers of innovation to learn new and better ideas, developing new insights into how we and other people think.

Yellow purges the heart of negative emotions. Sometimes people dwell on their fears and become mired in negativity. Yellow prompts us to grow our powers of intuition, enabling us to see the goodness within ourselves and others, opening up our higher abilities, sharing our love with all.

Yellow corrects the soul of diversions in its ultimate journey. Sometimes people are oblivious to their more noble possibilities and sink into pits of despair. Yellow empowers us to soar with angels, growing our inspirational abilities and ever closer to the wisdom of unconditional love.

Think and Heal

This third stage of personal growth is represented by our ability to make harmonious choices between our personal and social lives and to bring them together, creating a greater whole. Golden Yellow is the guiding light and its energy is centered in the Diaphragm Chakra, the area of the body that is vital to our breathing ability. Its nemesis, the sins of laziness and jealousy, may lead to poor balance with integrating our personal and social lives, resulting in the shallowness of chest breathing rather than the holistic wellness of diaphragm breathing. Yellow's Pure Love is waiting to help.

It has long been thought by many classical spiritualists and New Age writers that there is indeed a connection between the thoughts of our mind and the health of the body. Modern medical science may temporarily heal an unhealthy body but it has barely begun to address the problems of a disturbed mind, the pain of a broken heart, or the loneliness of an empty soul. In the same way that our physical bodies will age more rapidly if we don't follow a healthy nutrition and exercise program, our minds will also deteriorate more quickly if we don't continue to merge the best of our personal and social worlds. Healing, however, does require taking action. It means leaving behind outmoded behaviors and beliefs. It means using innovation and inspiration to develop new ways of dealing with life. Healing becomes easier whenever we use the personal power of a Golden Yellow Light and the partner within of Personal—Social—All.

FOREST GREEN
Radiating from the Heart Chakra
HUMAN—HIGHER—HIGHEST

Green is the fourth color in the light spectrum. It is the color of nurtured growth. We see green in the leaves of plants as they process the energy of the sun into matter for their growth. It is the color that nature uses to grow and multiply the life that sustains us all. In the political realm, some people refer to a politics that argues for a sustainable growth cycle that does not run on deficits, pollution and the highest possible profit margins, i.e., "green" politics.

This fourth partner is used for growing your 'human' decision-making abilities, your 'higher' social powers, and your 'highest' respect for all of Earth's life. By learning how to love others as you love yourself, you learn how to distinguish between your self-absorbed human powers and your higher social powers. And when you learn how to make decisions and live in accordance with your highest responsibilities, you not only learn how to balance what is right for you and the other people in your life, but you learn how to balance what is right for the rest of the world. A Forest Green Light—radiating from the Heart Chakra—will be your guide as you journey to the spirit of love, the energy that is both the singular and collective, the creator of all the awareness, intelligence, balance and goodwill that exists throughout the world.

For some partnership sessions, you may want to start off by contemplating each individual word of the introspections separately until you begin to feel the essence of the words. Other times you may find that chanting all three words together feels more comfortable. Your higher powers will guide you to what works best for you. As you continue your journey of personal and spiritual growth, the challenge is to maximize your strengths and minimize your weaknesses. This means seeing yourselves as an independent and unique human being while you are expanding your greater whole.

The Duality of Human and Higher

Repeat the word "Human" in a relaxed rhythm. Focus on a Forest Green Light emanating from your heart, defining the energy of your unique individuality in whatever manner you choose to direct it. You may find that you are mentally chanting these rhythms rather slowly. This is a sign that you are becoming absorbed in the practice.

Shift focus now to your breath, training your lungs to breath in rhythm with a pervading Green Light. Lengthen each breath now; draw in deeply as if you were breathing in the green, as if your breath was what allows you to absorb the power of green. When you inhale, draw the Forest Green into your mind. When you exhale, spread the light throughout your body, and then let it radiate out into the universe from your Heart Chakra, i.e., the heart, lungs and breast. In rhythm now, concentrate on spreading Green just as your blood is pumped and pushed by the pulsations of your heart. Green is one of the many colors that help you to distinguish and empower the uniquely human functions of your physical body, your intellectal mind, your emotional heart and your spiritual soul.

Add the word "Higher" to the rhythm now. The higher powers of awareness, ideals, compassion and respect flow across the planet like the civilizations that it has accumulated. Higher is the power of a society that balances itself in the search for prosperity and justice. Feel the higher power as you feel what it has achieved: tall cities and greater quality of life, art and culture; the virtuous goals of freedom and equality. It is an infusion of the energy from the vast desire of people everywhere who want to better the human condition. You may feel a lightening of your spirit when you connect to a feeling that love, desires, hopes and dreams are all human experiences, some easily achieved, some workable goals. Reminded that your life is just one part of this inexplicably vast drama, you will feel unburdened, even comforted by the feeling that the complexities of life are shared with all.

Resolution: Highest

From here, the Forest Green Light is accompanied by chanting the word "Highest," calling on Green's Pure Light, a light that wants to guide you individually and all of humanity collectively toward the best possible solutions. This is a critical stage in personal growth, where we move toward developing our spiritual powers. As we look to continue our journey, the challenge is to maximize our strengths and minimize our weakness. This requires that we see ourselves as independent, intelligent and responsible beings. This is where we can sort out the pros, cons, compromises and solutions that best enable us to go forward with our lives. By definition, Green's Pure Love shows us how we fit into the larger world of global stewardship so necessary for success.

The Functions of Forest Green

Green activates the body's commitment to achieving optimal health. It is the color we use to grow our instinctual awareness, giving new opportunities to evaluate our behavior and physical condition. It reminds us that to be in a position to take care of others, we need to be able to take care of ourselves. We cannot give what we do not have.

Green stimulates the mind's ability to construct knowledge from pieces of information. It is the color we use to bring segments of knowledge together to synthesize new and innovative ideas. Green helps us to see the beauty that resides within our intellectual abilities, thereby generating the circles of trust that forward the goals of all.

Green enables the heart's ability to plant the seeds of love that grow into loving relationships. It is the color we use to grow our intuitive abilities and to develop greater understanding for ourselves, and in turn, building loving relationships with others.

Green awakens the soul's evolutionary powers and sharpens our powers of inspiration. It is the color we use to grow our respect for the spirit of love, allowing it to permeate ever more deeply into our everyday lives. Green is the home of the collective goodwill of humanity, giving rise to the wisdom of all.

Love and Fear

Without the comfort of love, there is only fear. This fear can manifest itself in the depressing emotions of loneliness, sorrow, guilt and despair or the destructive emotions of hatred, jealousy, greed and revenge. Trying to alleviate these negative emotions, some of us may choose solace in material things. But these could never be satisfying because they cannot fulfill our essential social needs. Some people may escape fear by living their lives vicariously through others. Others may displace their fears by manipulating people through intimidation, dishonesty, bigotry or dogma. Still others may become slaves to the whims and shallow values promoted by peer groups or popular culture. Some may even abdicate their decision making to ancient faith-based belief systems that offer little or no relevance to the problems of our contemporary world. Without the compassion and empathy of Green's spirit of love, we will always have difficulty in making good choices and decisions for going forward with our lives.

Choice and Change

To love is to grow and change for the better in order to benefit ourselves and others. Life is always giving us opportunities to make choices and change. In an increasingly complex and diverse world, change is continually going on around us and, with the global advancement of the Internet, it is accelerating. This change should provide us an opportunity to reexamine ourselves and to see what is needed to continue our personal growth. But more often than not, this rarely happens unless we have a program to actively pursue it. It is usually easier for us to rationalize away the need to change because it is more comfortable to continue thinking and doing what we are used to. Usually, we only change when we are forced into acknowledging the painful results of our behavior.

Many of us fear change. But when we become immobilized by our fears, then our problems worsen. Excessive fear—or stress—actually changes the chemical and hormonal balance in our bodies. Fear stimulates a visceral "fight or flight" response when neither response may be appropriate. It releases excessive adrenaline into our system, further aggravating the stress. If this condition continues, it compromises our immune system and leads to the premature onset of illness or disease. This would surely be a warning sign that some of our behaviors, thoughts, feelings or beliefs are hazardous to our well-being, or worse, that we may have succumbed to the negativity of hatred and revenge. The heart, lungs and breast are the main physical areas that are vulnerable whenever we mismanage our opportunities to change and grow. Growth and change are always easier whenever they are guided by the partnerships of Human—Higher—Highest.

SKY BLUE

Radiating from the Throat Chakra

REAL—IDEAL—UNITE

Blue is the fifth color in the color spectrum light and our fifth stage of personal growth. People have always seen the sky as a sign. It told of weather, fair or threatening. It told of the favors and fortune of less perceptible things, like divine wrath or benevolence. The sky has also been the home of rainbows, giving inspiration for dreamers, artists and visionaries. The Spirit of a Sky Blue Light—radiating from the Throat Chakra—is our guiding energy as we practice this partner within. Blue's Pure Light is so profound because it is the only color that shines throughout the surface of planet Earth.

The sky offers countless inspiring visions. A clear blue sky will effect a person in ways they might not even recognize consciously; just adding a spring to their step or a sudden surge of energy to complete a task. It is Blue's Spirit of Love that will be our guide when we make the necessary steps of analyzing reality and sharing ideals as it is the sky that links us as one.

The success of this partnership depends on acceptance of the reality that we are all dependent on one another for our very livelihood and prosperity. It was once said that no human trait stays in style better than trust, and this is especially true in modern times. Although the "go it alone" mental attitudes are a part of the pioneering American life, they can be increasingly out of step with today's complex and globally interrelated world. Real—Ideal—Unite is where we turn when we are dreaming of a better life and a better world. This is where we seek to orchestrate the dreamer within us with others who share our dreams. For when the opportunity arrives, it is only by uniting with others that we can make our dreams come true.

The Duality of Real and Ideal

The Sky Blue Light is the power that you want to focus on. Once you are settled in a comfortable spot and have found the visual image of the color that works for you, begin to repeat the word "Real." Blue will be your guide now as your realistic abilities hone in on the key situations of your life that you have influence over. Reality is like a snapshot of the present that contains your realistic behavior and dreams but not your whims or fantasies.

After you are no longer voicing the word 'real' and are absorbed in the energy of blue, bring to mind your most important ideals and reenergize their rationality and functionality. This is where you will find the commitment and passion in order to merge them with reality.

"Ideal" is a powerful partner when coupled with reality. However, sometimes reality and ideals can be mirror opposites instead of being one and the same; most often they are somewhere in between. Repeat the word 'ideal' at a pace in rhythm with your breathing. At a certain point, you will find yourself no longer voicing this word, but being absorbed in the ebb and flow of its powerful energy, surrounded by a Sky Blue Light. Ideals turn negative when they are delusions of grandeur or they focus only on you. Your introspective abilities will sort out the truthful ideals from the deluded ones. Your ideals are up to you; they are the result of the choices you make. Blue's Pure Love will help you to learn the differences between your practical dreams and your unrealistic whishes. Real and ideal are now brought together by the word unite.

Resolution: Unite

Just chanting "Unite" alone starts the right energy, particularly if it is guided by a Sky Blue Light and a quiet introspective state. But there is farther to go. No one can simply will his or her real and ideal worlds together. You must discover, through the use of this three-word practice, the inner truth of your ideals. Truthfulness of an ideal is measured by its ability to benefit others. If your ideals are motivated by this truth, then they will be united to reality. By definition, what is true is that which is beneficial to all. Truth is manifested whenever reality and ideals are united by the power of Blue's Spirit of Love.

The Functions of Sky Blue

Blue is used to surround our problems and goals and to seek a greater truth. It teaches us that we must be truthful with ourselves in order to be truthful with others. Blue stimulates the physical abilities of the body; this helps us to see the world as it is rather than how we would like it to be.

Blue is used to evaluate our intellectual strengths and weaknesses. This is where we discover that truth does no harm and that truth will set us free. Blue awakens the intellectual abilities of the mind that help us to develop the best strategies for serving others so that we earn their services in return.

Blue is used to verify our emotions and discover our personal truths. It is truth that empowers our moral imperatives of humility, reason, integrity and charity. Blue invigorates the emotional ability of the heart; helping us to understand our personal self, giving us the insights necessary for continuing our personal growth.

Blue is used to look inside ourselves, to seek the rewards that are personal to us. Blue initiates the spiritual ability of the soul, helping identify the services that we truly love. And whenever we perform our services purely for the pleasure of helping others, it is an act of unconditional love.

Understand and Communicate

It has often been said that nature abhors a vacuum and truth and wisdom do not occur in one either. There is a fine line between true inspiration and mere illusion, between true innovation and simple imagination. Whenever we dream of something new that is only a benefit to ourselves, this is our imagination. However, if we dream of something new that can be a benefit to others, this is inspiration and intuition. Our best ideals come from working hard, acquiring knowledge, expanding our social network, and growing our personal powers of love. The body collects the information of reality; the mind analyzes it; the heart applies loving care; and the soul acknowledges the wisdom of the collective all. True instincts, innovations, intuitions and inspirations are the result of integrating input from our entire behavioral, intellectual, emotional and spiritual selves. Our brains have over one hundred billion neurons and our minds can grow over one hundred trillion synapses, but if left in the vacuum of laziness and ignorance, the brain will cease to grow and fail to develop its potential.

This stage of personal growth represents our uniquely human ability to accurately evaluate our human limitations, idealize our higher possibilities, and to bring them together with other people's goals. Sometimes our desire to bring our reality and ideals together can lead us to a new hobby. In time, avocations can grow into vocations, regardless of age. Once we have found what we really love to do, once we have found the services that reflect the best of our skills and talents, it is natural to enjoy doing them. Then the more we do what we love to do, the more we will be rewarded for doing it.

It is well within the domain of human powers to choose our thoughts and goals. But if we frustrate the metaphysical energy of this Throat Chakra by misjudging the truth—or surrendering to the selfishness of lying and stealing—our physical, intellectual, emotional and spiritual conditions will deteriorate. The result will be difficulties with communicating honestly and effectively. In time, physical disease will follow. Severe problems with analyzing, understanding and communicating our reality may show up as problems of the mouth, throat and vocal chords. These kinds of problems can always be addressed with a Sky Blue Light and the partnership of Real—Ideal—Unite.

OCEAN INDIGO
Radiating from the Brain Chakra
SERVE—TRUST—REWARD

Indigo is probably the cloudiest image when most people call the colors to mind. Between blue and violet, however, indigo is one of the seven colors of the spectrum of light. It is a distinct part of any rainbow. An easy solution for this introspection session is to have a color chart handy and to take a fresh look at indigo before starting. It is important to have a strong sense of this energy because this color helps us to look at, listen to, and learn from our world, just as people have long been drawn to the edge of the ocean to contemplate inner truths.

What we learn from this sixth stage of personal growth is that we are all in some form of a "service" industry, no matter if we are a manufacturer of goods or in a service occupation. What is more, how well we serve determines how well we will be served in return. The larger the network we serve and trust, the greater the rewards we will earn in return. All we need to do is look inside ourselves, visualize an Ocean Indigo Light—radiating from our Brain Chakra—and think about the three words of Serve, Trust and Reward. Soon you will be evaluating your memories, sharpening your mental acuteness, making distinctions between your thoughts and feelings, and learning to accept common goals.

The Duality of Serve and Trust

Locating a mental image of an Ocean Indigo Light should be seen as the "centering" practice of this partner within. Once you have it in mind, think about the word "Serve." Repeat the word initially with your inner voice, and then it will gradually become unnecessary to voice it. From the visualization of the color and the contemplation of service, you will see more and more clearly this truth: The better you serve, the better you will be served in return. This formula works for everyone. It works on the local level for you, your family, your friends and community. It works on the global level for nations accepting responsibility while seeking quality of life and a sustainable home for all.

We serve because we are part of a network of trust. Again, do not lose sight of the Pure Indigo Light; it is bringing the energy of Pure Love to your practice. Repeating "Trust" brings a vast array of inspirations to mind. If you find yourself adrift on mental images, refocus by returning to the Ocean Indigo Light. You might feel the weight of this color as a profound, vast, almost living entity like the ocean. The edge of the ocean, sea or lake, is a profoundly spiritual place where one can easily be taken in trance. Perhaps this is because the ocean is life; it is from the water that life first took hold on planet Earth. The color of indigo is not a shallow color field; it is as deep as the ocean itself. It is as networked as rivers are to lakes, as lakes are to the ocean. It is a continuous surface that flows with the boundless energy that is the collective goodwill of humanity.

Resolution: Reward

"Reward" is the unification of serve and trust and it is here that we want to remember that the hope of all beings is prosperity. Reflect with indigo on honoring the golden rules among all the colleagues and institutions with which you are involved, respecting others in the same manner as you would have them respect you. Then, through the use of the loving guidance of Indigo's Pure Love, you will improve your network of service and trust. Because we are all dependent on one another, and because we all need to be responsible members of the communities of Earth, we all need to continue to develop our trusting and servicing abilities for the rest of our lives. The inevitable result will be reward for all.

The Functions of Ocean Indigo

Indigo understands the behavior of the body. When we understand why we do the things we do, we will be in a better position to learn how to overcome our weaknesses and to reach our goals. Indigo guides us to trust the individuals who take the proper course with their lives.

Indigo inspires the thoughts of the mind. When we understand our mind's limitations, we learn to overcome challenges and to capitalize on strengths. Indigo leads us to the information that suggests new and creative solutions for our concerns and goals.

Indigo heals the emotions of the heart. When we learn how to separate our heart's positive energy of love from its negative energy of fear, we will be in a better position to evaluate the pros and cons of the relationships we are involved with.

Indigo guides the beliefs of the soul. When we discover our soul's reservoir of love, we become enriched by the collective energy of all, grasping a bigger picture of the common decency of mankind.

Listen and Learn

How do we learn to serve only those we trust? The ancient proverb "Fool me once, shame on you; fool me twice, shame on me" still applies. First, we cannot assume that we know who is right and who is wrong. We need to look to their bodies, learning their body language, collecting the information not verbalized. We look to their minds, learning the meaning behind their words. We look to their hearts, discovering their feelings and desires so that we can evaluate them for love and prudence. We look to their souls, learning from their wisdoms and beliefs, enabling us to strive for the information that is in the best interests of all.

One of the foremost benefits that come from serving others is that it then becomes easier to earn their services in return. Serving is an opportunity for learning, understanding and respect. Serving also breeds trust because deep down, almost all of us almost always want to do the right thing. Occasionally people make mistakes—selfishness and prejudice exists, tempers can be lost—but in the light of the billions of daily interactions between billions of people, they are remarkably rare.

Because the energy of our Brain Chakra is influenced by the genetic and cultural inheritances of our nature and nurturing, problems at this stage of personal growth could affect our abilities to think critically, evaluate alternatives and to listen and learn properly. Difficulties here can have an effect on the physical brain, the central nervous system, and its primary input systems, the eyes and ears. Problems would only be worsened by the sins of greed and rape. Headaches and insomnia would be among the more common warning signs. They can always be addressed by using the Spirit of Love represented by the Ocean Indigo Light and the partner within of Serve—Trust—Reward.

ROYAL VIOLET

Radiating from the Mind Chakra
PURPOSE—PEACE—BALANCE

Violet has the final position in our journey through the rainbow of light. It comes at the seventh stage in our use of partnerships of introspection. Once we have become accustomed to the practice of these seven, the eighth and beyond will be for pure spiritual growth. But first we need to grasp all the dualities that operate within the human experience. We need to sharpen our ability to focus on balancing our motivations for personal reward along with social and global goals. Working with a Royal Violet Light—a Light that radiates from the Mind Chakra—this partnership brings an expansion of love into our personal decisions and, with practice, into all aspects of our daily lives.

With Violet, we take our last step in the visual spectrum of light. Violet is our guide as people have intuitively used it for centuries to illustrate the pinnacle of authority, the King. The European thrones used violet in part because it had the most exorbitant cost of any ink at the time, coming as it did from octopuses in regions far beyond their control. Violet also enjoys the position of being the highest frequency of all of the colors of the rainbow.

The Duality of Purpose and Peace

Clear your mind of all distractions while relaxing in a place where you will not be disturbed. Visualize a Royal Violet Light. When you think of "Purpose," remember that this partner's term is neutral in itself and can apply to whatever situation you want to apply to it. Purpose, as you chant the term and absorb yourself in the rhythm of this duality, can be applied to simple issues of how to improve an ordinary day or to the more profound issues that apply to your family goals and your mission in life. As you are chanting you may find you no longer need to voice the word 'purpose,' but remember not to lose the regal color of violet that you are visualizing. Violet's energy is one of inner peace, the kind of peace that comes from spending your energy on a job you love or the nurturing of your family and friends.

Once you have stopped your inner voicing of purpose, start fresh with aligning the color violet to the "Peace" partner. The challenge of this partner is to not just relax yourself too far by chanting the word peace but to remind yourself that when you are at peace, you are at your best. If you remain focused on the Royal Violet Light as well, you will begin to open this purpose and peace partnership up to its true expression: A personal peace that results from each individual member working together in social harmony. Peace is the reward of a society that is governed in the best interest of all. Peace is the reward that will come to you by putting your own individual talents to that collective good. So how would you function best in a global society? By managing your talents, whatever they may be, and by doing what you do best. Peace will be the reward of living the life you want. Global awareness will bring universal peace for all.

Resolution: Balance

Now chant the word "Balance" while immersing yourself in Violet's Pure Love. When you move into this balancing phase, the unified partners of purpose and peace, feel free to return to the subject of your fulfillment. What you will discover when you find balance is that it comes from a peace that results from having a meaningful purpose in life. Soon you will obtain a better understanding of what brings forth comfort for the body, contentment for the mind, affection for the heart, and guidance for the soul. Never forget that it is healthy and happy people who also make the world a better place just by balancing their purpose with the goal of peace for all.

The Functions of Royal Violet

Violet is for strengthening the body's commitment to a healthy perception of reality. We use its power to give comfort to others, earning comfort from them in return. But sometimes people mistake material things (e.g., jewelry, cars, houses etc.) as a source of solace, beauty and pride. But if these items are not shared and appreciated by others, they leave us feeling empty and alone. Then all the energy poured into their creation or purchase becomes a waste of time and wealth.

Violet is for enhancing the mind's ability to pursue lifelong learning. We all have the ability to broaden our intellectual knowledge, thereby enabling ourselves to teach as well as learn. But sometimes the mind creates fantastic and complex ideas that are of no value to anyone and then they become an exercise in futility. An over-specialized intellect may enable brilliance in one topic and yet decrease the ability to know the essentials of a wider base of knowledge.

Violet is for developing the heart's capacity to cultivate the passion to be the best that it can be. We utilize its power to care for others so that we can be cared for in return. But sometimes the heart mistakenly makes emotional commitments to the wrong people, institutions, clans and/or belief systems. Although we may receive a powerful sense of belonging from being members of a group, if the group's purpose is not for the benefit of the greater whole, then these misguided emotions turn into frustration and misfortune.

Violet is for forwarding the soul's potential to grow closer to the ultimate power of pure love. We use its power to sharpen our wisdom as well as to learn from the wisdom of others, thereby bringing peace to all. Alas, sometimes the soul gives in to the selfish will of others and if we seek to forward other people's goals, we relinquish our own unique truths. This may result in cults and extremism, and sometimes rivalries and war. The abdication of our purpose to others may lead us to floundering in meaningless directions.

Inside and Out

In this seventh stage of personal growth, we transcend our personal limitations so that we can purposefully improve our lives, the lives of others and bring peace to all. This is the stage that represents our premier ability to grow. This is where we achieve a peace that comes from knowing our reality and understanding our inner self while maintaining purity of heart and clarity of vision for others. This is where we achieve 'balance' by entering a place deep within ourselves where our personal human powers combine with our universal higher powers. We enter this space freely chosen—not mapped out for us by others—a place where we are truly at ease with ourselves and our world. The inevitable result is that this is where pure love awaits. It shows us how to save ourselves, and perhaps, help save the world.

A Royal Violet Light is the guiding spirit and its energy radiates from our Mind Chakra, the energy of the cerebral cortex located near the top of the head, the ultimate pathway to Pure Light and Love. If we are comfortable with all of the first seven introspection partnerships, peace and good health will result. However, from a metaphysical standpoint, it is believed by many that any obstacles in the goal of utilizing all of our personal powers could affect the Mind Chakra and hence the cerebral cortex, the immune system, or any of the other major organ systems. Sever problems with the mind chakra may even deteriorate into the worst of all deadly sins, terror and murder. But these are the evils that the Royal Violet Light and the partnership of Purpose—Peace—Balance is particularly adept at eliminating.

LORD—GOD—DIVINE
Western Spirituality

This partnerships and the next two use the cumulative power of all of the colors of the rainbow, they are unfettered by any sin and they will be guided by a Pure White Light. In addition to the visible spectrum of white light, these partnerships may also operate among light's higher frequencies that are invisible to the human eye. Here, we begin to step into the realm of the non-visible, the energy realms that are beyond the perception of normal human experience. These are the energies that scientists refer to as ultraviolet light, x-rays, cosmic rays, and a vast unknown of energy and matter. When you practice these last three partnerships, picture a Pure White Light, a light that emanates from no one source but illuminates everything perfectly. This is the light of the Lord—God—Divine, a light that casts no shadows.

On the nature of the Pure White Light, little may be said with certainty. Indeed, in the frequencies of energy beyond our physical perception, there may be a power that humans do not easily understand. Perhaps Pure Light is a channel for the extra-sensory perceptions that can have such a profound impact on our lives. In any case, we have to accept the fact that humans are still on a journey of discovery. Although we may be limited to the animal sphere, with the practice of these last three partners, we seek to open our lives up to the highest frequencies of the universe where possibly Pure Life, Love and Light reside. Even though we may not fully understand these spiritual powers, we still need to engage them because they can be very useful in helping us to chart our unique pilgrimages toward a better awareness of ourselves and our home, the planet Earth.

The Duality of Lord and God

Focus on building an image of a Pure White Light in your mind. You will know when you have the right image because you will find it easy to keep it in your head. Now begin by chanting "Lord," a partner who will function as a guide for your brain's behavior and thoughts, its feelings and beliefs. This Spirit will make itself available when called. Chant this word quietly but at an even pace. You may find that as you become absorbed by this powerful partner you will not need to voice the word anymore. You are receiving the help of the Spirit of Lord, a power that stems from Pure Light, a power that improves your normally pre-judged decisions, a power to be active in the realm of your human world.

Now, partner the Lord with "God." Chant this word with the conviction that God is love, pure and simple. This is the spirit of your higher powers, your ability to want what is right for yourself as well as the other people that are involved in your life. Now it is the Spirit of God that wants to guide your personal awareness and ideals, your compassion and respect. It is a stimulus to your ability to understand and empathize with what is right for all of Earth's life. By developing the power released by this duality of Lord and God, you will be integrating both human and higher functions into all of the ambitions of your dualistically-powered life.

Pure Light Meditation: Divine

While verbalizing "Divine," visualize a Pure White Light bringing forth new spirituality for all of the contrasting aspects of your human nature. Divine is the poetic equivalent of all the kindness and integrity of the universe, the immortal power that creates new instincts from your body, innovations from your mind, intuitions from your heart, and inspirations from your soul. Meditate on the power of this Spirit of Divine; it comes from a pure love that cannot betray. Whenever the Lord resides in your body and mind and God manifests in your heart and soul, then the power of the infinite Divine will guide your uniqueness and determination, your intellect and compassion, your reality and intuition, your understanding and respect, the multifaceted skills that Western traditions associate with "will."

The Functions of Lord—God—Divine

This partnership is all about Love, Pure and simple. We see it in the human traditions of selflessness, understanding, empathy and respect. It is the caring feeling that extends itself to all beings and is free from any attachments. In today's world, Pure Love is expressed in the many kind acts that people do for the benefit of others. It is demonstrated whenever we open our hearts to the people we know and to the ones we don't. It is manifested by those who share the rewards of their endeavors with their families and forgo personal pleasures in order to benefit loved-ones. It is the extended family that supports, respects, nourishes and honors its members. It is witnessed by the kind neighbor who is willing to share and lend a helpful hand when needed. It is defined by the citizens who are involved in issues, vote in elections, and support the political activities that build a global society that provides equal rights for all. It is the employers and employees who recognize they are in business to serve the needs of others. It is found in the institutions that focus on their specialties and yet are willing to work with other institutions in order to support a common good. It is the community that abides by just laws, respects minorities, defends human rights and is willing to make sacrifices for the good of all. It is the governments that take responsibility for their constituents and support the moral code in their borders and beyond. It is the nation-states that support modernity, opportunity, prosperity and equality. It is in the realization that people can build a better world by solving the local problems that others ignore. It helps individuals forgo immediate gratification and to save and invest wisely for long-term goals. It is the recognition that there is a delicate balance of energy in this world and that one must be a conscientious consumer. It is the workers, intellectuals, artists and visionaries that help define the higher values of our faiths and cultures. It manifests in the rescue workers and public servants, the everyday heroes who sacrifice their personal safety for those who are in need. It is the ability to accept our mortality and the fact that all physical incarnations will end. And finally, this love within is the belief that our souls have meaning and purpose that it will live on and on.

Love and Wisdom

This is an excellent partner that we can turn to whenever we need help during the course of a normal day. It is particularly helpful for the Western mind because, if nothing seems to be going right, or if something in the real world has just gone wrong, all we need to do is close our eyes for a few seconds, repeat this partner within, and then tune into the spiritual power of Pure Light and Love. Sometimes solutions arrive immediately. Other times they may appear later when we have returned to our daily routines. But whenever we engage in any of these three-word partnerships, however briefly, we build a buffer zone between ourselves and the sometimes all too negative human powers to which we are periodically exposed. Eventually, the solutions of Pure Love will manifest themselves when the time is right.

At this point in the introspection sessions, we should be well on our way toward more effectively managing our unique human and higher powers. In these final three sessions, we are striving to further the Spirit of Love that reflects the goals of all. This is where we merge the traditional Western powers of Lord and God with the universal powers of Divine. This is where we complement our personal powers with the highest powers of all.

Reminiscent of the Western traditions of Father, Son, and Holy Ghost, we only need to think and act with the wisdom traditions that are available from the Spirits of Love and the partner within of Lord—God—Divine.

MALE—FEMALE—SPIRT
Eastern Spirituality

This partnership corresponds to a further complexity of the interaction between the dual aspects of our personalities. But, before we start this practice, it is important that we accept the possibility that the universe may contain more spiritual beings than those that we are familiar with. If so, when you invoke this chant, an "amazing grace" of male and female energies will become available to you. This grace may come in the form of guardian angels or spirit guides. Or possibly they come in the form of patron saints, deceased ancestors or the various forces of nature. Remember, although we need them more than they need us, they want to help. Whether they actually do help is for you alone to decide. All you need to do is talk to them and to be willing to listen for their guidance. (Some Christians may find it beneficial to substitute the invocation of "Jesus—Mary—Grace" for this partner within.)

Obviously, it is in everyone's nature to have many dualistic abilities; clearly we are distinctly separate sexual beings. But our species has inherited a long history of focusing males and females into different roles. For millions of years our male predecessors specialized in hunting and gathering activities while our female predecessors were more likely to be involved in the nurturing of children and related social behaviors. However, in the modern world, there is no reason why all of us cannot learn how to bring the best of our male and female aspects together. So set aside any superficial opinions you may have about the pros and cons of gender differences and simply enjoy the wonder and diversity of all aspects of human life. All it takes is a little introspection and meditation and, with the help of spiritual beings, we can bring together the best of both.

The Duality of Male and Female

Once you are settled in a quiet place, focus on clearing your mind of any conscious images by visualizing exclusively with a Pure White Light. Draw in a few large breaths before beginning to chant "Male." Soon, you will be able to bring forth a spiritual being that is available to guide the male-like aspects of your nature. This type of spiritual being specializes in logic and intellect. It has a "down to earth" analytical orientation. It analyzes behavior and responds to reality. It specializes in deductive reasoning, discriminating and step-by-step sequential thinking. It takes a straightforward approach to analyzing data. It is goal directed and likes to focus on one thing at a time. But with specialist dominated thinking, there is a tendency to compartmentalize everything. Then the world becomes separate blocks of knowledge that can lead to difficulty in forming broader perspectives and seeing the inter-relatedness of different parts.

Once you have an impression of how these male-like characteristics function in your life, proceed directly to chanting the word "Female." Here, you will find a spiritual being that is available for guiding the female-like aspect of human nature. This spiritual being will be more interested in emotions. It is a generalist. It has a holistic orientation and appreciates the bigger picture—the relationships between different features. It is able to embrace ambiguity and make connections between disparate facts. Because it is comfortable with inductive reasoning, it uses an "out of the box" style of thinking. As it is also the home of loving guidance and intuitive powers, it is more likely to see solutions in a broader social context. However, with generalist-dominated thinking, there is a tendency to overlook details and misread reality. This is why we need to meditate for the optimal balance between both aspects of this male-female duality.

Pure Light Meditation: Spirit

Now it is time to begin the "Spirit" meditation. This request may bring forth spiritual beings that are likely aware of what you are asking of them. But, as this is an acquired skill, you may not be receptive to them until you have practiced several sessions of this introspection/meditation. Your request may bring forth two distinct spirits, representing the different aspects of the male and female characteristics, or it may bring forth a single androgynous (genderless) spirit, one who is capable of helping out with both aspects of your male and female duality. In any case, be receptive. Some spiritual beings have an incredible ability to blend together all of the contrasting aspects of your personality. Feel your love for them and you will feel their love for you in return. Meditate alongside these spiritual beings as they offer a pathway to a pure Spirit of Love.

The Functions of Male—Female—Spirit

In this partner within, we seek the optimal unity between the male and female aspects of our lives. Whenever we increase the communication between our intellect and emotions, our analytical and intuitive selves, we open ourselves up to the full array of our human, higher and highest potentials. These energies in turn bring forth new and creative insights into our body's behavior, our mind's thoughts, our heart's feelings, and our soul's beliefs. Understanding and uniting these abilities is the essence of creativity. If they are not in harmony, it is easy to become frustrated and unbalanced. But when we bring them together, we become fully engaged in the moment, challenged to do our best, motivated by passion, and united with the common goals of all. We feel exhilarated and alive.

Choose and Learn

One of the foremost benefits of looking at the opposite aspects of our personalities is that it affords us the opportunity to make choices and to learn from them. Choice is the underlying basis of our decision-making ability. By making new choices we will experience new outcomes that are not always predictable. Sometimes they produce the results we want but other times they do not. Either way, making new choices always gives us new outcomes and opportunities for learning. The ability to choose starts from the ability to look at opposites. It is in our "awareness" where we look for the optimal choices between change and no change, our extrovert and introvert selves, the old and new aspects of our lives. It is in our "ideals" where we seek what is right for our analytical and intuitive sides, our left and our right, our cooperation and innovation. It is in our "compassion" where we look for balance between the short and long term, the parts and the whole, the liberal and conservative. It is in our "respect" where we contemplate the bigger pictures and seek the proper balance in our personal yin and yang: the harmonious interplay of the opposites of the universe. Regardless of what choices we are evaluating, they are always easier to make whenever we invoke the Pure Love of spiritual beings to help us out.

Escape and Addictions

However, our choice-making abilities may be easily disrupted by an abnormal imbalance in many of the various aspects of human nature. Without the guiding influence of higher powers, it is easy to escape into behavior patterns (or sins) that are harmful to our well-being. Addictions, for example, frequently arise when we seek immediate gratification as compensation for a lack of fulfillment in any of the four behavioral areas of life. For instance, the energy of the body may be wasted through addictions to sex, violence or self-mutilation. The energy of the mind can be squandered through addictions to laziness, drugs and alcohol. The energy of the heart may be exhausted through fearfulness, living vicariously through others or failing to open its ability to love. The energy of the soul can be destroyed by an absence of purpose, the pursuit of other people's agendas, or an addiction to risk and gambling. One only needs to walk through any casino to see all the sad and lonely faces.

Many times we wind up squandering our potential by failing to travel the evolutionary paths in front of us all. To make use of all of the energies of our lives, we need to be ever mindful of the spiritual reward available through the use of Eastern traditions and the spiritual powers of Male—Female—Spirit.

LIFE—LOVE—LIGHT
Global Spirituality

The final stage of these last three introspection/meditations focuses on calling on all of the global traditions of pure life, love and light. Free from any regional differences, these are the transcendent truths behind our motivation to do what is right for ourselves, the other people we know and love, and for all of Earth's life. They are the energies that bond us together in society. They are revealed in our reverence and compassion for the intricate web of life that sustains us all. They are in our personal force that empowers us on our journeys, expands our possibilities, daring us to be all that we can possibly be. And as our lives are only on loan to us, with this loan comes a responsibility to make our lives and our world a better and more bountiful place for our children and for all.

With the power of Pure Life, Love and Light comes a trust that these powers resides at the very center of our being, as it is at the center of the universe. It is the power behind the beginning when a singularity of Pure Energy turned into particles and particles turned into matter. It is the love and energy behind the "Big Bang" when energy and matter bonded together and created the elements of life. It is the power behind the "elective affinities" that bond atoms, creating the heavier elements and thereby more complex molecules. It is the love and energy of complex compounds that partner together to form the amino acids, proteins and DNA molecules that are essential for the advancement of life. It is the power behind the evolution of the plants and animals that gave rise to the evolution of the human race. Everything has developed from this single spark of infinite energy that had a burning desire to evolve. Pure Love is the insatiable desire of all things in the Cosmos to improve. It is the universal and eternal power that is at the very heart of all that is. Its power is ever growing and compounding.

We are all sons and daughters of energy. It is from energy that we have evolved and it is toward energy that we are evolving. This progression is only a matter of time. The human race is but a single species sharing a single planet in one of the billions of galaxies scattered throughout the known universe. Genetically, we are all brothers and sisters, gifted with the power of trust, working together with the aim of one world and one goal: A world guided by the universality of the Spirits of Pure Life, Love and Light.

The Duality of Life and Love

Focus your mind. Empty it of the daily stresses and worries. Silently chant the word "Life."

As you relax deeper, the energy of a crisp 'Pure Life' replaces the simple word life. It glows from darkness, sometimes pulsing in short bursts with the pounding of your heart, sometimes radiating with the hum of your brain. This is the Energy of Pure Life that emanates from no one source, but everywhere at once.

Shift focus now to your breath, training your lungs to breath in rhythm with the energy of Life. Lengthen each breath now; draw in deeply as if you were breathing in the energy, as if your breath were what allowed the energy to increase. When you inhale, you draw the energy into your mind. When you exhale, you spread it throughout your body, relaxing the muscles. In rhythm now, concentrate on spreading the energy throughout your body, just as your blood is pumped and pulled by the pulsations of your heart. Pure Life is energizing your thoughts and feelings, empowering you to do the right thing for yourself and others. What you will see next is a beacon of Love.

Add the word "Love" to the rhythm now. Allow the warmth of love to be drawn into you when you inhale, feel the desire of wanting to share this love to others when you exhale. Now you have gained access to the Spirit of Love, a pure and selfless expression for all the love and kindness the world has ever known. Focus on a love so pure that it creates love whenever it is called. Pure Love's essence is unconditional; the joyful desiring of what is right and best for all of Earth's life. It is an absolute love of infinite proportions that cannot betray. Allow this duality of life and love to stimulate your higher powers of awareness, ideals, compassion and respect, empowering you on your journey to do what is right for all.

Pure Light Meditation: Light

Just by chanting "Light" you will have entered a deeply private space, perhaps a place inside yourself that you have never been before. Initially, you will experience an "energizing" sensation when you enter into this deepest state of mind. Then you will feel a flood of empathy when Pure Light and Love become one with the ever-present now. Your soul will reach for this purest of loves, a universal love that wants what is right for all.

Here, the triple powers of the universe wait. When you succeed in partnering the powers of Life—Love—Light together, to the exclusion of all other thoughts, you are developing your whole-brain's highest love, a love that is capable of pursuing the most elusive of goals, seeking what is best for all. Concentrate on the power and meaning of these three simple words for as long as you wish.

You will feel a profound sense of peace as the love and wisdom of the universe enters your world. This energy will penetrate deep inside you as all of the contrasting aspects of your human nature come together in a partnership that produces loving insights into how to best manage your life. At some points, you may want to bring a problem or goal to mind. While focusing on your life, allow the Spirits of Love to offer new insights and solutions. The love that emanates from these introspective and meditative partnerships will help you find the creative new solutions that benefit not just your own self-interests, but also the interests that bring better global awareness, leading to a greater good for all.

The love released by these partnered dynamics calls on the collective goodwill of all humanity. Drawing upon this global goodwill, it allows a better understanding of your personal strengths and weaknesses. It allows you to gain new insights into your reality, intellect, emotions and spirit. Sometimes, answers will come immediately to this state. Other times, no new thoughts may be immediately apparent, but with practice they will appear steadily over the course of time. Either way, these solutions are simple insights into what should be done about your concerns and goals. However simple the answers sometimes are, they are nonetheless very important: they allow you to go forward with your life. And the more we bring Pure Light and Love into our lives, the faster we will evolve from simple human love, a love that is limited to what it finds lovable, to unconditional love, a Pure Love that wants what is best for all.

In this life, searching for the sacred aspect of the Divine is half the battle, but only the beginning. The more difficult achievement is to let the Spirits of Love guide us throughout our lives, thereby making this a better world for all. All it takes is a little awareness and appreciation for the partner within of Life—Love—Light.

The Partners Within

PART II

GLOBAL SPIRITUALITY

Perhaps the best way to begin my explanation of meditation and global awareness is to share with you some of my personal experiences. I grew up in the America of the 1950's. My family was deeply bound to the traditions of the Roman Catholic Church. Naturally, as a youngster I did my best to please everybody and I certainly tried to adhere to the practices and beliefs of the time. But I remember many nagging doubts about what was going on. The prayers and rituals seemed to be intended to empower the church as the main guardian of righteousness. Yet their concept was narrowly defined by reverence for God. Approaching my priest in a confessional when I was troubled by a difficult issue I faced, or just a fear that I held, I was told that for my sins to be forgiven, I had to get on my knees and say ten "Our Father and Hail Mary" prayers and that the answers always lay with God. It was then that I realized that the traditional orthodoxies were stuck in an impersonal, dogmatic past. What can a priest who responds to a child's fears with a prescription of "hosannas" have to offer for the difficulties of the psychology of common people?

Not only was it not working for me, it certainly wasn't working for many other people in my community. People were complacent with the fact that they were forced to say one thing but do something else. The result was to accept a kind of personal failure in the recognition that one wasn't as godly as the pastor was supposed to be. To accept this failure is to accept the hypocrisy of the Church. It is also to resign yourself to not growing into all that you can be, spiritually. And there were precious few alternatives to the traditional Christian churches in most people's neighborhoods. It was either them or the godless mess of secular society.

While growing up I was also awed by the frightful global scenarios that unfolded before me through a regular reading of the *Time* and *Life* magazines. The atrocities of WWII and the Korean conflict morphed into the cold war and an arms race that eventually produced the absurdity of a nuclear firepower equivalent of over one hundred tons of TNT for every man, woman and child on the face of this earth. In the midst of all the insanity, I can still remember thinking that surely there must be a better way.

During my college years in the 1960's, I, like many others of my generation, first became aware of the Eastern theologies of meditation. The contrast was startling. Not only was the emphasis on listening and going inside oneself for answers but there was a near total absence of faith-based belief systems built around an all-powerful monotheistic God that directs what happens to the world. To this day it never ceases to amaze me how the human race continues to have two entirely different approaches for personal spiritual growth.

Although I practiced several meditation techniques, I never achieved the self-mastery that many Easterners, who grow up practicing, are able to achieve. Apparently, the window of opportunity for achieving world-class physical and mental skills seems to narrow substantially when human beings begin their third decade of life.

More breakthroughs awaited. These lessons were hard bought by my generation. In the 1970's, we saw the development of the popular non-fiction genres of self-help and personal growth. The "Big You/Little You," "The Inner Child," and the "I'm Ok, You're Ok" brands were an essential break with the "old" model that the truth lies in orthodoxy. Sadly, all they seemed to have given the world was the rise of the "me" generation of the 1980's, which is famously remembered for the absurdity of Gordon Gekko's classic line "Greed is Good." I saw firsthand how ugly the self-interest of the rich, hell bent on getting richer, could be. That is when I decided to re-approach the practice of meditation. Although I may never be able to achieve the deep intensity of meditation that Eastern monks obtain over a lifetime of practice, I did make one remarkable discovery: *Sometimes it only takes a few seconds to have a "Gamma" moment that can change the direction of your life forever.* Other times changes evolve more gradually over a period of time but with practice and commitment, you too can discover new meaning and purpose for your life.

About *robertcfelix.com*

As a retired stockbroker with over 40 year's experience, I have been acutely aware of the ups and downs of American and global aspirations. I have watched the remarkable surge of Western economies and more recently, the stunning rise of emerging ones. Over the decades, I have seen the rise and fall of entire technologies and industries, of currencies and derivatives, of amazing human aspirations and spectacular failures. And I have observed war and peace in human societies and the nations we create. For us to survive into the 21st century and beyond, we will have to be wise and worldly in deciding right from wrong, good from bad, love from fear, and trust from doubt.

Over the past fifty years, we have seen the world create more wealth than has ever been created in the entire history of mankind. Over the next few decades, we have the potential to double this wealth, and then double it again. But I am worried about the future of the children of our world. Historically, global exploitation of limited resources without global governance has been a recipe for disaster.

Look at our future. The world's oil supply is set to peak in this century's second decade. And the land and water resources; both are increasingly being exploited to near their limits. The air temperature and quality needs to enable a healthy population, not risk it. The relentless ascendancy of rampant empires is the greatest risk for our future. Over the course of history, we have seen the rise and fall of many a nation; most have come and gone, but none has yet been able to govern all of Earth's life. Hopefully, what is different this time around is the Internet. It enables nearly everyone to be a witness and a participant in our global future.

Fortunately, human dignity is bigger than the governments we create. People are pretty good at getting along with their friends, families and colleagues. But it is crucial that we grow beyond our regional interests, beyond the lack of understanding for strangers, and beyond the little respect we have for cultures other than our own. What will enable this growth is the realization that for our very salvation and prosperity, *we are as dependent upon others as they are dependent upon us.* This is the goal of The Partners Within: global spirituality and unity for all.

First we need to master the ability to use introspection. Then we are ready to take our journey to the next level through the use of meditation. This is where we achieve the joyful state of entering into loving partnerships between ourselves, the other people involved in our lives, and by extension, all of Earth's life. And this next step uses the understanding of one of the most important dualities of all: the one of *brain* and *mind*.

BRAIN AND MIND

Throughout this book, I use the term "duality" to describe how two contrasting traits comprise the opposite ends of a theme. A common example is "good" and "bad." These two forces are at the extremes of a spectrum called "morality." A duality can be any issue that comes with contrasting characteristics or differing points of view. The key to understanding dualities is that they are not just about a simple contest between two forces. Just as world history has often swung from progress, to chaos, to reform, and then to progress, so too daily life is a balancing act of our dualistic natures.

A more striking example may be found with life itself. Life comes in two basic varieties: plants and animals. We see these two forces as the primary duality of the world that we live in today. They represent an illustration of how two entirely different organisms have evolved into symbiotic relationships by sharing a mutually beneficial goal of survival. Plants and animals have co-existed on our planet in a balanced partnership of equals for billions of years.

In your own life you may readily identify dualities as two related yet contrasting forces that may operate in harmony, or sometimes not. For instance, knowing how your emotions make separate demands from what you logically know to be true, you achieve balance. Part I of this book detailed how you can achieve the many balanced partnerships that produce increasing self-knowledge and personal growth. But in Part II, I want to detail a central scientific concept: the duality of brain and mind.

Incredibly, it wasn't until the beginning of the 21st century when Western scientists began to seriously study the *mind* as being something other than just a *brain*. The concept of the mind had been largely dismissed as unknowable because it was too difficult to quantify. Thus, the scientific study of the human mind stayed in its infancy and trying to understand its function was mostly left to philosophers and theologians. Further, most scientists believed that once people became adults, imbalances of the mind were only treatable with surgery, electro-shock, and/or powerful mind-altering drugs. Very few scientists dared to think that they could show people how to change their brain and mind for the better.

But thanks to the advances in computer tomography, 21st century neuroscientists are converging on a two-part theory of brain and mind that they like to describe as the duality of the *structure* of the brain and the *function-*

ing aspects of the mind. In short, according to this theory, the brain "structures" our information and experiences while the mind "functions" during our daily lives. Hence, the mind is considered the "learning" potential of the physical brain that we "think" with. Why is it that, although we may bring a lifetime of experiences into our present day, how we "think about" our experiences is far different than "learning" from them? The important point is that these are two separate and distinct forces.

What has become fascinating to scientists is how the mind seemed to "emerge" from the structural aspects of the brain. And now scientists are discovering that the mind's functioning aspects can in turn change the structure of the brain. For example, neuroscientists have shown that stroke and accident victims, people who have had brain damage formerly believed untreatable, can make remarkable progress with the functioning aspects of cognitive-behavior therapy. This is the phenomenon that they refer to as the "neuroplasticity" (or better yet: neuro-*elasticity*) of the brain. In this book, it is referred to as "learning."

The Partners Within technique is a new tool for reprogramming the normally fixed structure of the brain by partnering it with the potentially more dynamic functioning aspects of the mind. Any human being who chooses to continue to think and learn proves that the brain and mind can have mutually rewarding partnerships even though they are as different as the definitions of structure and functioning imply. Although the majority of learning occurs in the first two decades of life, all an adult needs to do is practice a skill and, over a period of time, the brain restructures itself while the mind learns new functions. The acquisitions of the skills of introspection and meditation are but a few examples. Our thinking and learning are far from being fixed, regardless of age.

What follows, then, is the philosophy of how the brain and mind are used for the thinking and learning aspects of our lives. In short, the brain thinks about how it has structured its past so that it can compare it to the learning potential of the mind. By using this duality, along with pure love, you can manually—and without drugs—reprogram both your brain and mind for the better. And the latest evidence suggests that this dynamic can continue throughout our lives. Yes, you can teach old brains new tricks.

Dualities illustrate how we form our personal identities by organizing the brain and yet we are able to remain flexible by using the creative aspects of the mind. Now let us look at how they are distinct.

The Brain

The human brain is comprised of over *one hundred billion* neurons (nerve cells). The working definition of the brain is that it is the physical organ that processes sensory inputs and stores information and experiences. It thinks about how to structure (organize) itself so that it can prioritize personal and social considerations and responses. Because each of us has had a unique past, our brain attempts to make sense of it so that hopefully we can function at our best. This structuring starts with making sense of events by organizing them along behavioral, intellectual, emotional and spiritual/cultural lines. Over the years, we build various platforms of pre-determined responses to different situations. Sometimes they are realistic and logical ones but other times they can be stubborn or naive. For example, your brain processes the words you are reading on this page and it may accept, modify or reject them depending on what else you may have learned or what you were taught in your past. The results could also be a rethinking of your individuality and consequently, your outlook on life. The substance of your personal introspections will help you reflect on what you have learned in your past, helping you to decide between which decisions worked best and what may need to be revised. It starts with thoughts, the precursor to intellect.

The Mind

The mind in cognitive (consciousness) science is something altogether different: The human mind can create over *one hundred trillion* synapses (electro-chemical reactions) between neurons. They start as feelings, the precursor to emotions and holistic responses. The mind is the word for the human abilities of recognizing realities, making intellectual connections, empathizing with others, and abstract/symbolic thinking about the common good of all. It forms patterns and reacts to changing conditions. More often than not, it is easier for the brain to use its pre-determined responses and much of the time, we discover that these responses are working just fine. But the mind can also be aware of changing conditions and hopefully make new, more practicable decisions. Other times, we find that the brain has become "fixed in its ways" and reluctant to change. But our mind should have the ability to evaluate the relative merits of situations and then to figure out the best balance for all. It is part of our free will. The goal of meditation is for both the brain and mind to be operating simultaneously in a balanced "partnership of equals" throughout our daily lives.

The beauty of this brain-mind duality is that it affords us the gift of choice, learning the most appropriate response to the duality of brain and mind is one of the most basic ones. We have the freedom to choose what we think about and how we want to behave. We all have this skill; it is a gift of human life. We can make choices between what has happened with our lives and what we want our lives to be about now. After all, our brain and mind are unique to us and we are the only ones who could possibly understand the most personal aspects of our lives.

So how do these dualities help us make better decisions? Keep in mind, although both your brain and mind can operate along side each other, most of the time it is always easier to think about what we have learned in our past rather than learn something new. But this potential duality of brain and mind offers an opportunity to open us up to different sides of our issues. If you find conflict, then you should seek the solutions of "what's best for both," the most balanced solutions for all concerned. Then it becomes easier for your resolutions to be a reflection of the realization that we are all in this together; resulting in more globally responsible you.

Dualities are a springboard for opening up a dialogue between our thoughts and feelings, our thinking and learning abilities. They capture the essence of a self-empowered ability that comes from deep inside us. This is where our brain enters into a personal dialog in order to observe the merits of our behavior. Our mind then evaluates the pros and cons of the social situations and strives for the solutions that are in the best interest of all. By meditating along with a pure white light, we will be in a better position to identify and discard the destructive emotions that are harmful to ourselves and others. Remember, virtually anybody can do this because it is as simple as structuring introspections and functioning with meditation. The result will be an improved ability for evaluating behavior, looking at the different sides of issues, balancing the brain and mind, and achieving a greater use of pure love.

We all have a responsibility to consider the results of our lives. This means reviewing the quality of what we are doing. It is through the use of these deeply personal partnerships of brain and mind that we build a better position to understand what is uniquely within our human potential and what our higher possibilities might reveal. And whenever we look to the power of what is right for all, we will be on the path for achieving the highest of responsibilities, citizens of Planet Earth.

TWO VIEWS

As we race forward into the 21st century, mankind's unlimited ability to prosper will be increasingly testing the Earth's limited ability to support that prosperity. Over the past 60 years, our global population has tripled from some two billion people to over six billion. Simultaneously, the global middle class—defined here as those who have discretion over thirty percent or more of their income—has increased ten fold, from three hundred million people in the 1950's to over three billion in 2010. The combination of global trade (of goods and services) and global wealth (people's net worth) have also risen exponentially, from a mere trillion dollars in the 1950's to well over one hundred trillion dollars in 2010. Incredibly, in the coming decades, these numbers have the potential to double again. Demographers and economists estimate that by 2050 there will be nearly ten billion of us and that over seventy percent will be global middle class or better. Trade and wealth together could easily be approaching $500 trillion. The human race is very good at making money. What we do with our accomplishments is far more difficult. Forever more, we will not only be looking for the proper balance between our individual wants and needs, but for the proper balance between our aspirations and the limitations of our only home, the Planet Earth.

And how do we find that balance if people and nations continue to put self-interests first? The United Nations is one example of a global community trying to balance development while limiting the demands of increased consumption on the Earth's finite resources. But we cannot wait for a global bureaucracy to solve this problem. The power to balance growth with resource sustainability resides within the personal choices of each of us.

Up until now, most of us have been focused primarily on what is right for ourselves and what is right for the other people involved in our lives. Little consideration was needed for the people that lived on the other side of the globe. But today we live in an increasingly interconnected world and sometimes our need to specialize in our local tasks makes us short-sighted about what is going on in the rest of the world. Unfortunately, our personal goals can blind us into the "us versus them" situations that often end with tragic consequences.

As we rush into this new century together, we are going to need to look at all aspects of the issues we face—not just the tradeoffs between "limited and unlimited" but at the very essence of the differences between "you, me and we." The "Two Views" offered below cover a broad range of human issues where there is no single answer. Liberal and conservative political opinions are a common example, especially in America. Both views are relevant. Different people can have different opinions and still be decent people. These differing viewpoints are traditionally regarded as dualities, (or more fluently as "issues,") because they represent contrasting, yet acceptable aspects of the human experience. But to too many people, their views are often framed as right and wrong, or black and white. Yet when we look at populations as a whole, we see many shades of grey. People can be liberal in some areas of their lives and conservative in others. Normally, we all have the ability to be flexible in our views, but frequently we are not. Too many of us go about looking for the information that supports our views, and wind up refuting anything that contests them.

But recognizing that there are lots of changes going on in our world—like the relentless competition for natural resources, trade, profits and global growth—means that we should be reviewing our positions more frequently. We all have the ability to look at both sides of the issues we face. We need to learn not only what other people are thinking but why they think their way. Two Views gives us a convenient introspective and meditative tool for a better understanding of the elements of balance that our dominant species needs. After all, we only have a single home to share. Hopefully, a better understanding of the following 'two views' will put us in a position to see not only what is in our own personal best interest, but what is in the best interest of all.

Nature And Divine

From ancient myths to the modern realities of the human race, many of us have held that there is a duality of Nature, which represents the knowable world, and the Divine, the spirit of love. Nature enables energy and matter to combine and produces life. It then persists in the creation of new qualities through mutations while natural selection favors of more effective ones. The Divine is the keeper of a higher source: the laws of energy and balance of nature; our social order and moral truths. Like the duality of reason and faith, we only need to contemplate the interplay between Nature and Divine. Then we will see the incredible possibilities for the ever-growing circles of trust that propel the human race forward.

History And Prehistory

Historians define history as the advent of writing systems that represent language. As such, our oldest written histories date to around four thousand years ago. However, prehistory for humans reaches back over millions of years. Before writing came the abstractions of hunting, stone tools, fire and social groups. The art and myths that come to us from ancient peoples represent the viewpoints of an enormous variety of human thought and feeling. On the other hand, the writings of contemporary religious traditions, which occurred in earnest between one and three thousand years ago, collected the local beliefs of specific tribes and regions. These writings became fixed into the "sacred" scripts we have today. But by looking for a balance between the two views of historical and pre-historical, we see the immense cultural diversity available to the human race today.

Faith And Culture

The difference between these two views is that faith is used for our sacred-spiritual beliefs and provides answers for the mysteries of life. Culture is used for our secular real-world beliefs and works to organize and unify groups. Faith allows us to suspend disbelief and enter into the realm of mysticism where the absolutes of morality, trust and truth exist, known here as pure love. Culture is more worldly and, due to the changing needs of societies, is constantly being modified by reason and laws. Both terms are used as belief-systems that societies use with the goal of making the most out of society and life. They provide the answers to the issues we're unsure about so we don't have to figure everything out for ourselves. Both faith and culture evolved over the millennia and were intricately involved with the evolution of agriculture, civilization, industry and information. But now, at the dawn of the Global Age, both faith and culture need to continue to evolve. It is essential that we learn to balance our sacred beliefs with the realities that surround us. And then someday we will truly become a nation of nations, a prosperous home for all of Earth's life.

Unique And Common

What are the strengths and weaknesses of humanity? What are my personal strengths and weaknesses? Each of us is created by a unique DNA molecule that assembles the proteins that generate our physical, intellectual, emotional and spiritual energies. Although 99.99% of our human DNA is common to all other human beings, there are around 300 million molecules in our DNA that are uniquely arranged for each individual, and that is why no two of us are exactly alike. And, in addition to the possibility of random mutations, each of us has also had a unique nurturing experience. Because of the changing challenges of modern families, times, residencies and daily life, even identical twins do not turn out to be identical. By understanding our uniqueness, it enables us to put together the best of our realities, intellect, emotions and beliefs. By understanding our commonality, we discover balance in determining what is right for ourselves and what is right for all.

Big And Little

This double metaphor looks at the many different points of view that may arise between different spatial perspectives. Big is synonymous with other people, the public and the many. Little identifies the self, the individual and the one. For instance, what is the difference between a Big Church and a Little Church? The Big Churches are in the neighborhoods that surround us. They are the communities where people go to be with like-minded people and to share commonly established beliefs. But a Little Church also exists solely within you. It enables you to discover the unique combinations of your nature and the nurturing that defined you and no other. Our Big Church offers beliefs for the societies we live in. Your Little Church is exclusive to you. It is where you go to find the proper balance between yourself and your world.

Top And Bottom

From the top-down dictates of the "powers that be" to the bottom-up actions of "grass-roots" movements, looking for balance between these two views is essential for the challenges of the modern age. Most of us spend most of our time specializing in our individual skills and careers. Sometimes we work at producing goods and services. Other times we oversee resources, regional and global interests. Some times we govern, other times we are governed. We always need to govern ourselves. Most of the time we function well, other times we stumble, we can always start over. Sometimes we put together enormously complex sciences, organizations, governments and cultures. Other times we are contributing participants. Nobody can be an expert in everything. We'll always need to work with everybody involved and to trust that those around us are also working toward mutually beneficial goals. Most of the time, they do. We need to be responsible, trustworthy, transparent and accountable in our actions. Whenever anybody isn't, it is the responsibility of everyone to get involved to see it right. Like all of our views, we need to consider the pros and cons of both top and bottom in order to discover the best results for going forward with our lives.

Trust And Doubt

Trust is the default mode of humans. Studies have shown that trust plays the most important role in socially-oriented species, of which no better example exists than humans. If we hadn't been able to trust family and friends when we were growing up, we wouldn't be here. As a result of being raised in a mostly trusting environment, almost all of us almost always want to do the right thing. (Fact: Global incarceration rates are far less than 1 percent of the population.) Naturally, we also expect responsible behavior from the other people involved in our lives. But in a global environment we also need to extend our relationships to the individuals, communities, institutions and governments that surround us. And due to the local differences of natural resources, climate, social structures and regional cultures, not everybody shares the same goals. That means most of the population is like "strangers in foreign lands." Doubts arise whenever events occur that are not in the best interests of all. From one end of this duality's spectrum to the other, all we need to do is look at the different sides of this issue and we will see that we are all inextricably involved in this life together. Then by looking for the proper balance between trust and doubt, we will see what is right for all.

Local And Global

Up until the past few centuries, we have been largely a local society. Most of our lives revolved around getting to love and trust the family and friends that were within walking and talking distances. And as we lived within the golden rules, our societies flourished. But now the human race appears fated to enter a new reality as we expand to some ten billion over the next few decades. The rights of the individual will need to be increasingly balanced with the rights of the whole. Likewise, nations will continue to maintain their cultural identity but will need to be increasingly united in global goals. The problem is that people find it easy to love and trust those that they are familiar with. But they are generally neutral toward anyone they don't know and are quick to turn negative toward anything that appears foreign or different. Social scientists have shown that human beings are pretty good at becoming friends with up to a few hundred people in their lives. But for almost everyone, getting much beyond this number is more complicated and we simply run out of time and abilities. Typically, the rest of the human race becomes an unknown quality. Bit we have only limited opportunities if we restrict ourselves to the use of local friends and family. As we open ourselves up to the global possibilities through the use of politics, treaties, business contracts and cultural respect, then the reciprocal altruisms of beneficial goals will flourish.

Short And Long

Time is the issue we are looking at here and the viewpoints are about how we differentiate between the short and long term. Usually, we do our jobs and tackle our more obvious projects on a daily basis and most of the time, that's fine. But we need to take a few minutes out of our days and think about the long term consequences of what we are doing, why we are doing it, and what other people are doing. Internet searches tell us about what other people think and why they think their way. There are a lot of long-term changes going on that are unfolding gradually and they are of a subtle variety. Some of these major changes may be developing beyond our personal life's expectancy and these changes are easy to ignore. But most of the goals we face are of both a short and long-term nature: education and business opportunities, safe and healthy living conditions, social safety nets for the aged and infirm, and responsible financial systems and governments are but a few. Our technological prowess may have exploded but our politics have not. Over the past fifty years our global economy has created more wealth than had ever been created in the history of humankind. Now, with a free enterprise system trading over $60 trillion of goods and services per year, there is ample resources and wealth to do the right thing for ourselves as well as for future generations. Our moral compass is simple: If it isn't right for the children of this world, we shouldn't be doing it.

Earth And Life

Have you ever wondered how our finite Earth, which has only limited land, air, water and energy, can continue to support a life that knows no boundaries? Earth is a single host, a collection of limited resources. Life is the energy that takes those resources and multiples itself. Historically, mankind has gone to war whenever resources ran short. A sad fact, but rather than fighting, we should be looking at building a better way. Fortunately, humans have incredible brains and are far more talented than anyone has ever imagined. Most of us are aware of the advantages of getting along with the people involved in our lives. Success breeds success. But soon, for the first time ever, the human globalization of our planet will necessitate that we take a critical next step: balancing not only what is right for ourselves and the other people we know, but balancing what is right for all of Earth's life. And where will we find this balance? It comes from a God/Divine trust that we're all in this life together. With global dominance comes global responsibility. Nobody can deny that we are all involved with one another, and together, responsible for our very salvation and prosperity.

Most of us don't live in monasteries. We live in a real world that is globalizing at accelerating speeds. We cannot continue to be committed to the "old ways." We are very good at economics. Now we need to do as well with our political, social and cultural programs.

THE "EASY CHAIR" PRACTICE

Meditation does not require an extensive command of technique or any religious training whatsoever. Anyone with an open mind can tap into this higher potential. Time spent with these efforts is time spent opening yourself up to new abilities that start from within you. Initially, your effort may be a matter of simply reading through the meditations. Some days you may want to reflect on your personal challenges. Other days you may want to think about your goals. Once you begin discovering the unique and personal aspects of your personality, you will soon be finding the potentially rewarding solutions for your life, bringing new meaning and purpose to your practice.

If done on a regular basis, the results may begin as simple thoughts or feelings that help you go forward with your life. At the very least, it is an easy relaxation technique that opens your brain and mind to new and better solutions that may pop into your head during some later time. Take these subtle changes in perspective and attitude and multiply these benefits times five to seven days a week, year in and year out, and you will see how it works. Be advised, however, that your dreams may change in an instant but your reality may change more slowly over time. But with commitment, bringing your human and higher powers together with the highest powers of all, you will have many opportunities to transform your life. And you can get started in as little as a few minutes a day.

THE SESSIONS

Mornings, before breakfast, are ideal times for meditation because you can always make whatever it is that you hope to accomplish for that day the purpose of your session. Evenings are a good time to reflect upon the events of the day, on what went right or wrong, or to seek answers on how to improve. Because almost all of us have busy lives, it is also possible to have mini sessions during the course of the day. Even on the busiest of days, it only takes a few moments to close your eyes and reflect on the purest of meditations: light, love and one. This will set a proper frame of mind for better solutions as you return to the tasks of your daily life.

If you are having difficulty visualizing the seven colors, it may help to use the color chart on the front cover of this book, or possibly, try using a triangular glass prism. Hold the prism up to the sun or a bright light and slowly rotate it so that you can observe the seven colors of the rainbow. Stop at each color and memorize it by closing your eyes and concentrating on it until that color is thoroughly etched in your mind. It only takes a few seconds for this intense beam to enter your brain and create a lasting impression.

After reviewing any of the meditations, you may find some specific areas where you will want to focus your attention. Keep in mind that many people will have difficulty growing their higher powers while problems and conflicts remain in their human realm. If this occurs, you may want to address the most relevant issues among your dualities until you reach a sense of comfort with them. Then use the colors and words for more intensely personal solutions. This structure allows for flexibility and customization to respond to the changing needs that everyone will experience over time.

Although you may start your practice in as little as a few minutes a day, eventually you will want to grow your sessions to longer periods of time, perhaps fifteen minutes or more. The partners within were designed with basic purposes in mind and with the hope that eventually everyone would be familiar with them all. The more you practice, the more likely you will be able to find the areas which are most important for you. Sometimes you may choose to use them like a prayer, reciting the words while thinking about how they enlighten your concerns and goals. Once you have brought the limitations of your human powers under your control, you may even want to move through each word with as little as a single breath. Then you can spend extra time on the Pure White Light meditations, which are the most powerful for pure spiritual growth.

The Colors

Throughout the ages, the color spectrum of visible light was used for meditation, as people must have long wondered about the properties of rainbows, appearing as they mysteriously do, usually after some unusual weather patterns. Several thousand years ago, Hindu theologians assigned each of the seven colors to seven different "Chakras," their term for seven different energy centers of the physical body. Here, the colors and a modernized version of chakras are paired together to work to locate different problems and goals of contemporary life. The chakras are used for both the introspections of Part I and the meditations of Part II offered below.

Today, many New Age writers and holistic practitioners are converging on the idea that certain personal problems may indeed result in physical problems in these different energy centers of the body. It is also my observation that the greater the disparity and/or conflict between the different aspects of people's dualities, the more likely a physical problem will result in its corresponding energy center. If you are suffering from a malady in any of the physical areas associated with these centers, this would be an indication to spend extra time on that color and its accompanying meditation. The usual sequence is introspection first and then meditation for deeper understanding. Meditating with the colors and these seven classic metaphysical energy centers can be especially effective for a better understanding and balance for any of your behaviors, thoughts, feelings, and beliefs.

The Light

After reviewing the colors, you will also want to use the Pure White Light for spiritual growth. This will mean different things to different people at different times. Many will want to use the partner of "Life—Love—Light" for both an opening and closing meditation as it is the purest and most universal of all. Consider this example to be an apprenticeship to the insights offered by all of the partners within. From only this simple little three-word phrase, you will be well on your way to bringing an ever-increasing amount of relaxation for your body, introspection for your mind, meditation for your heart, and resolution for your soul.

Note that the relaxation and introspection techniques offered below are similar to those of Part I. They are expanded here with a more in-depth explanation in order to prepare you for the more intensive meditations that follow. However, if you are going through a particularly difficult time of your life, where nothing seems to be working, you may want to skip down to the "Big and Little" chapter below. It offers help for those deeply troubling times in our lives when everything seems to be going wrong.

Relaxation for the Body

The first step is to put your world on pause and to relax your body. You need to become perfectly still, totally alone with the pounding of your heart and the hum of your brain. This is where you will be free from the roles you play that ensure your survival; free from the demands of the people and the institutions that absorb your daily life. This is where you will discover a place for you alone: the home of your unique inner self. In this place of deep relaxation, you begin the work of creating a balanced partnership of equals between you and your world.

To enter into an intense meditative state, you will need to find a quiet spot where you will not be disturbed. The first objective is to totally relax your body. Draw as many deep breaths as necessary to relax all of your muscles. Start with your feet and work your way up to the top of your head. Focus on the pulsations of your heart and the rhythm of your breath until your mind quiets down and you have settled into a relaxed and peaceful "easy chair" state: spine straight, head effortlessly resting on the shoulders, feet on the floor and palms comfortably upright on your lap. This begins the empowerment of your human, higher and highest journeys. With practice, this ritual will help you to obtain a state of deep relaxation within moments.

Introspection for the Mind

Once you have entered into a relaxed state, this is where you review the memories, pictures and stories of your life while observing the results of your behavior. Allow the power of introspection to illuminate the pros and cons of your recent actions. Soon, you will be able to recognize the differences between your love and fears and your trust and doubts. Do not judge, simply become an impartial observer and accept them as they are. As you enter into a personal conversation between the multiple aspects of your personality, let the dual energies of your brain and mind flow independently and freely. Your brain represents your behavior and thoughts; your mind empowers your emotions and beliefs.

Now, think about a concern or goal that is important to you. Sometimes solutions become evident by simply recognizing the source of the problem. Other times answers do not come immediately but later after you have returned to your daily routines. Solutions may even come in the form of dreams—night or day. Occasionally solutions come in startling new revelations that change the direction of your life. More often you will find a simple new thought or feeling that helps you go forward with your unique personal journey.

At times, you may want to intersperse your concerns and goals while repeating some of the meditations that are most meaningful to you. All you have to do is immerse yourself in the world of a partner within and then allow the words to expand throughout your consciousness. With practice, these beautiful words and feelings will nurture a new and better you.

To all sides of the concerns you face, give each the freedom to express themselves as unique aspects of you. Be careful to not be critical or judgmental. Simply allow the unique aspects of your personality the liberty of individual self-expression. It only takes a few minutes to uncover some of the potential conflicts that linger below the surface of your everyday consciousness. Remember, these are the aspects that are unique to you. In order to uncover them and to seek resolution to any of your personal imbalances or conflicts, you are the only one who can look at and listen to your inner, personal self. Nobody can do this for you but you.

After a few minutes of letting the thoughts and feelings flow freely, the next step is to enter into a meditative state. This is guided by all three words of the meditations offered below. This is where you allow the Spirit of Love to help you learn what is best for all of your personal dynamics.

Meditation for the Heart

Traditional Eastern meditations depend on years of self-training and mind-bending discipline. Indeed, many Eastern masters frequently practice eight hours a day or more. The Buddha himself is quoted as saying that enlightenment is a "non-attainment" state. What he meant is that with meditation, insight and enlightenment do not come in "visionary" experiences, but as a result of a lifetime practice. It is these traditions that Westerners have so often profoundly misunderstood. It is little wonder that many people are disappointed when they try meditation. But it is also in the spirit of Buddha that the partners within work. Although they are also seeking inspiration from a lifetime of practice, by partnering introspection and meditation together, learning and insights can come in as little as a few minutes a day.

For meditation, I am offering some of the meditations based on my earlier book, *Three-Word Meditation*. They follow a sequence of color, action, and object. They are presented here for readers who would like to bring their practice to a higher, more intensive level. They are easy to learn and they offer a quick way of moving through the partners within technique. Note that, although they use the same colors and chakras of introspection, they also use a simpler form of self-imagery that still articulates the identity of brain-mind partnerships. Their function is to help you identify the source of your concerns so that you can stimulate the compassion of pure love for your life. As the functions of color never leave these meditations, these three words work especially well for more deeply intensive sessions. The chief determinants as to which set you may want to use is dependent upon the availability of your time, the difficulty of your concerns, and the complexity of the goals you are attempting to solve. Feel free to go back and forth between any of the introspections or meditations that apply to your current situations.

Resolutions for the Soul

The partner within of Life—Love—Light (from part I) works well for both warming up and closing down meditations. Sometimes you may want to use it to simply bask in the glory of Pure Life and Love. Other times you may want to let yourself become immersed into the universal beauty of Pure Light. You are capable of entering into all three states of delight. The more you practice, the more intense your compassion and understanding becomes.

Eyes closed, silently chant the word "Life" over and over again until you eliminate all other thoughts. Then, picture the energy of Pure Life starting to glow from the inside of your mind. Pure Life is the energy that wants what is right, that wants to survive and prosper. Gradually slowing the timing of the chant, switch your focus to the rhythm of your breath, using a single breath for each chant. As you inhale, expand the energy of life inside your physical mind. As you exhale, visualize life radiating throughout your body: torso, arms and legs. Concentrate on the energy of your life glowing and radiating throughout your entire being.

Now, immersed in the energy of life, chant the word "Love" with the same rhythm that you obtained with the word 'life.' Concentrate on a feeling of pure and selfless appreciation for all the love you have ever known. Allow the beautiful warmth of love to sweep over you as you are about to open yourself up to the different colors of the Spirit of Love. Love's essence is unconditional; the joyful feeling of wanting what is right and what is best for the other people in your life.

By chanting the word "Light," Pure Life and Love now become one with your personal God/Divine, one with all of Earth's life. Here, the triple powers of the universe wait: Pure Life for your human left-brain, Pure Love for your higher right-brain and Pure Light for your highest whole-brain. These partnerships stimulate the growth of universal and unconditional love, a love that is capable of pursuing the noblest of goals: seeking what is best for all. Concentrate on the power and meaning of any of these three words for as long as you wish.

Now, having warmed up to a deeply compassionate state, it is time to use the power of color to explore all of your personal energies while contemplating the following meditations. Initially, you may want to read through the following paragraphs to get a sense of each. Then you may want to practice with whichever three-word phrase that seems best for your current situation. Soon, you will be able to easily visualize the colors and chakras and then, by simply remembering any of the words, you will create your own personal partnerships of Pure Light and Love.

Red—Being—Me

Visualize a Brilliant Red Light, radiating from your Pelvic Chakra, strengthening the foundation of your torso. Let the Spirit of Red bring out the best of your total being, bringing you to a better understanding of who you are and what you are doing with your life.

Orange—Clean—Past

Visualize a Fire Orange Light, radiating from your Navel Chakra, empowering the digestion system that energizes your life. Let the Spirit of Orange clean the negativity from your past, bringing global spirituality and harmony with yourself and the world.

Yellow—Heal—Now

Visualize a Golden Yellow Light, radiating from your Diaphragm Chakra, empowering the deep breaths of relaxation that heal your life. Let the Spirit of Yellow unlock your understanding of the ever-present now, gaining acceptance of all that is.

Green—Grow—Trust

Visualize a Forest Green Light, radiating from your Heart Chakra, strengthening your cardio-pulmonary system and, in turn, growing your desire to be the best that you can be. Let the Spirit of Green grow your understanding and trust for the intricate chain of life that supports us all.

Blue—Serve—Bond

Visualize a Sky Blue Light, radiating from your Throat Chakra, sharing your services with others while earning their services in return. Let Spirit of Blue show you the way to bond with others by demonstrating this truth:

The better you serve the better you will be served in return.

Indigo—Words—Learn

Visualize an Ocean Indigo Light, radiating from your Brain Chakra, learning from the opportunity of words. Let the Spirit of Indigo guide you to the mutually beneficial agreements that define what is best for yourself, other people and all of Earth's life.

Violet—Peace—Joy

Visualize a Royal Violet Light, radiating from your Mind Chakra, helping you to learn what is best for your personal peace. Let the Spirit of Violet show you the way to joy by using this fact: We are but a single species sharing a single planet and we need to do what is right for all.

While continuing to remain quiet, non-judgmental, and receptive, allow the spirituality of pure love to permeate your life. Soon, you will enter into a deeply personal space that exists somewhere between resting and sleep. You will feel an "energizing," "tingling" or "light-headed" sensations bristling throughout your being as you enter into a pure meditative state. Western Science has confirmed the reason why countless generations of people all across the globe have searched for this state. It is the "gamma-band" brain wave that does not rely on conscious thought or waves of emotion. Scientists have shown that meditation enhances this unique brain activity and stimulates the areas of the brain where happiness, understanding, compassion and goodwill reside. From the human brain's newest pre-frontal cerebral cortex to the ancient depths of the emotionally laden limbic system, your whole brain will sparkle with electro-chemical activity. This is a far different mental state than the introspective "alpha" brain waves of the normal active-alert state. This is the place where the Spirit of Love brings together the thoughts and feelings of your life, empowering you to learn new and better ways of understanding. This is the place where you will find the "gamma" moments that change your life for the better.

Here, in this very special state, the creative dynamics of all of your human abilities will be released. You will be on the plane of the three inter-related powers of Pure Life, Pure Love and Pure Light where the proper balance for all of your partnerships will be revealed. Ultimately, the harmony of this triple power will fuse all of your energies into a personal, and thus uniquely true, "human-being." The love released is like a beacon calling on the collective goodwill of humankind and the Purest Powers of all.

The love of your internal partners will emerge as a moment when you are totally "one" with all. This allows you to see your personal life and recognize how you have lived it. The joyful merging of all your partners, thanks to the provocative insights of this simple journey, is the essence of a partner within practice. These cherished partnerships will reveal the relationships that lead to what is best for you, the people you love and work with, and what is best for all of Earth's life. Remember, although there are no magic formulas, the key to success is simple: *practice*. The most important stories of your life have yet to be told.

Every person has the ability to bring about a better world for themselves and others. Many people pursue the classic religious virtues of their cultural/spiritual heritages and those practices continue to be held in high regard today. But you also have to make a conscious choice to explore your personal inner self. Think of it as entering into a moment between your thoughts and your reaction to those thoughts. It is like listening at a crack in the door that opens you up to the power of the Cosmos. It is in this "gap of silence" that the whispers of the universe come to you through an opening to your soul. Even if you enter this moment for only a few seconds, it is here that your partners within will reach out and touch all the Pure Light and Love that the universe has to offer.

Genius, Thomas Edison once said, is 99% perspiration and 1% inspiration. Introspection is the alpha, the perspirations of time. Meditation is the gamma, the inspirations of the ever-present now.

THE FOUR FUNCTIONS

S o how do we go from the duality of brain and mind to the power of three-word meditation and then wind up with the "four functions" of the body, mind, heart and soul? Good question. In short, whenever we are alone with the reality of our thoughts and feelings, this is where we see that we are at least of two minds about our world. At a minimum, most of us recognize the differences between our past and present, our head and heart, our self and others and our life and loves. To these most basic dualities, the partners within add a third element: others—either people or spirits. Being social animals, we strive for partnerships with the other people that are involved with our lives. When the partnerships produce what is best for all, the results reward us in the form of better understanding and awareness for the four distinct functions of every human being.

The reality of the body,
The intellect of the mind,
The emotions of the heart,
The spirituality of the soul.

(Please note there are two definitions of "mind." First, there is the mind part of the aspects of the brain/mind duality that we have been talking about here in Part II. But there is also another definition of "mind": the one associated with the four functions of human energies known as the physical body, the intellectual mind, the emotional heart and the spiritual soul.)

So how does understanding these distinctions help us to improve? The comprehension of the uniqueness of our four functions is a necessary step that needs to be taken in order to gain a broader understanding of the full potential of all of our human energies, thereby furthering our personal self-awareness as well as the awareness of our global responsibilities.

The body, mind, heart and soul are distinct aspects of the human experience that should be operating smoothly together. This is not to say that we are made of four separate beings. The reality is that we are all comprised of a wide variety of strengths and weaknesses within each of these four functions. The problem is that some of these functions may wind up competing with each other, resulting in confusion. Or worse, one function may dominate and overwhelm another function, leading to unbalanced decisions. But when we use the partner's technique to see how the energy of our four functions can be clarified and balanced, then we will see how they help improve our daily lives, the lives of others, and ultimately, all of Earth's life.

First, in the realm of human powers, our body, mind, heart and soul operate in the secular world whenever we function through the use of our behavior, thoughts, feelings, or beliefs respectfully. By evaluating how well these functions are performing in our lives, we gain new insights into the areas of our personality that may be in need of attention. Then, it will be easier to see the resolutions for the conflicts and goals of these four components.

Next, the discoveries made through the use of our higher social powers will translate into new and better advances. These are the results that produce new awareness of our surroundings, new ideals for mutual goals, new compassion for the people in our lives, and new respect for the greater good of humanity.

And finally, whenever we turn to our highest spiritual power, we will be rewarded with new instincts, innovations, intuitions and inspirations. With these powers, our body will achieve peace and security; our mind will find stimulation and fulfillment; our heart will develop love and compassion and our soul will discover meaning and purpose.

There are twelve components of the body, mind, heart and soul identified in the table below. To use these components, you need not memorize them; rather, consider returning to this section periodically after you have become comfortable with the partners within technique. Your introspective and meditative abilities will only continue to grow if you do.

	HUMAN		**HIGHER**		**HIGHEST**
BODY →	Behavior	↔	Awareness	↔	Instincts
MIND→	Thoughts	↔	Ideals	↔	Innovations
HEART→	Feelings	↔	Compassion	↔	Intuitions
SOUL→	Beliefs	↔	Respect	↔	Inspirations

For the purposes of understanding the four functions outlined here, we are going to assume that every human action, thought, desire or conviction can be examined in light of these four general classifications. Understanding how they act *independently* of each other helps us to better understand our individual strengths and weaknesses. Understanding how they act *collectively* helps us to understand our total person, or how we relate to ourselves and to the world. Understanding these four autonomous functions can be especially helpful for analyzing and evaluating the areas where we should be concentrating our efforts for maximum personal results.

Daily Life

- The body functions as our behavior. It is the result of participating in the real world, with all its economics, hardships and pleasures. In its pure human power form, it is limited to the five physical senses. In its higher form, it brings us new awareness about our surroundings. In its highest form, it is referred to as our instinctual abilities. These are also known as our "sixth sense," "gut reactions," or "extra sensory perceptions" that are the functions that alert us to new and better ways for dealing with our unique selves as well as the realities we are involved with.

- The mind functions as our thoughts. Our thoughts enable us to understand the rules, roles and politics we play in our personal lives and in our careers. It works with bargaining our skills, understanding our professional life and dealing with the organizations that we are involved with. The limitation of the human side of our mind is that it is often limited to its existing knowledge base. Our higher mind strives for new ideals for cooperation and mutual goals. Our mind's highest powers include our abilities of innovation, enabling us to think more originally and creatively.

- The heart functions as our feelings. Our feelings can grow into personal relationships, helping us to bond with others. The problem with the simple human heart is that it often confuses its positive and negative emotions as both can be equally powerful. Our higher powers seek better understanding and compassion for these emotional challenges. Our heart's highest powers enable us to receive new intuitions about all our relationships, identifying better solutions that improve our interactions with others.

- The soul functions through our beliefs. It is found in the spirituality that we use in attempting to deal with the mysteries of life. It strives to understand the metaphysical-theological questions that have no answers. It represents the goals and visions that we have for our future. Its human shortcomings, however, include the shortsightedness of the sometimes questionable values and beliefs of prevailing faith and cultural systems. Our higher powers teach us to respect ourselves as well as the goals of the other decent people in our lives. The inspirations of our soul receive their power from the collective goodwill of the Spirit of Love.

Self-Analysis

One way to begin self-analysis is to consider how well the four functions are working together. Problems often arise when one aspect dominates the others, thereby limiting our options in dealing with life. For instance, many of us are frequently faced with the dilemma of having to decide between our intellect and our emotions, between our selves and others. The goal of self-analysis is to not only learn how to better understand and manage our personal life but to also learn how to further the growth of our social life. Most people have built some working knowledge of what they are good at and what they struggle with. Indeed, we all have the ability to learn lessons about ourselves from everyday experiences. But it is necessary to take another step by understanding how the separate functions of the body, mind, heart and soul interrelate in our life. Evaluating each of these from our human, higher and highest potential helps us to discover what is working in our life and what is not. By evaluating these twelve components, we will be in a better position to understand the unique combinations of our personal strengths and weaknesses as well as the strengths and weaknesses of the people and institutions that we are involved with.

Pure human power can be very self-serving. Although individuals exercising raw, unbridled human power can temporarily achieve great heights in positions of authority, those ruled by it are inevitably frustrated. Sometimes leaders under the sway of their selfish human powers can be enormously destructive to themselves and others. Germany's Adolph Hitler, Cambodia's Pol Pot and Iraq's Saddam Hussein are just a few of history's more horrific examples. A worst case example occurs when Al Qaeda members allow their emotions and beliefs to overwhelm their behavior and intellect, resulting in terror and murder. Eventually, however, justice prevails because there are far more decent people in this world who harness their human powers for beautiful acts of civility and righteousness.

Most of the problems that we encounter in our daily lives are directly related to the dominance of human power over higher power. However, no one can function through higher power alone—the fact that human beings will always be animals is indisputable—and it is our human powers that enable our comfort and security. But the primary reason for learning to enhance our higher and highest powers is to learn how to properly direct our lives so that we advance our wisdom and vision of what is right and good for all.

Reality and Intellect

Although human beings have four separate functions, two of them, the body and mind, could be considered components of the left hemisphere of our cerebral cortex, i.e., the "brain" of brain/mind. The body is most interested in reality. Its priorities are the behaviors that support survival and comfort. The mind's thoughts strive to analyze and to figure things out. Together, the body and mind represents what is known here as the realist/intellectual side of our personality. It looks at reality from a historical perspective by using its prior convictions, or it attempts to forward its intellect by acquiring new information and knowledge. Both are basic human powers because they can operate entirely on their own.

For instance, some people have achieved an enormous amount of wealth and power by pursuing their personal goals solely through the use of their raw human powers. Indeed, it is not unusual to find individuals who appear to go through life evaluating everything in terms of "what is in it for me?" They become focused on the reality that they find themselves involved with and then attempt to forward their personal goals with little regard for others or a greater good. Sadly, many others may be trapped in the routines of the roles they inherited or their behavior may be dominated by their "lower" powers such as ignorance or hate-based belief systems. The result for these people can be lives of isolation, poverty or sometimes reactionary fervor. And if any of the evils of the "deadly sins" prevail, darkness descends and everybody suffers.

Emotions and Beliefs

The heart's emotion is considered human love whenever we feel positive feelings coming from inside us. The soul's beliefs consist of the faith and culture that we inherited and modified over our lifetimes. Together, the heart and soul represent the "mind" (of brain/mind), or the right side of our cerebral cortex, the listening-learning-holistic side of our personality. Our heart is our ability to take good care of ourselves and others; it is our desire to love and be loved.

The limitation of simple human love, however, is that usually it only loves that which it finds lovable and generally, it is apathetic to everything else. Human love also needs to be nurtured and if it is not properly developed, negative emotions are the most likely result. Then, this emotion may turn a destructive will toward anything that it finds foreign or unpleasant, leading to hostile acts that eventually cause the destruction of the self, as well as others.

However, when we turn the energy of the heart and soul in the direction of unconditional love, we have found the passageway to our most potent spiritual powers. Humans are certainly capable of pure love but we do need to work at it. For those of us absorbed in the reality of self-survival, it does not come easily. But thanks to the combined possibilities of our heart and soul, we can be united with the collective energy of all the goodness, love and intelligence that exists throughout the universe. Then it is through our highest power that we find our personal connection to the guidance of Pure Love. We may choose to remain lazy and ignorant and then eventually we will be left feeling empty and alone. Or we may use our introspective and meditative abilities to seek the instincts, innovations, intuitions and inspirations necessary to find the brighter possibilities of our lives, which would benefit our entire being and all.

Building a pathway to the spirit of love is a personal process whereby we use the power of partnerships to bring an ever-increasing amount of unconditional love into our lives. We enter into this process not only to better manage our personal human and higher powers but to put ourselves in a better position to deal with the unique personalities of others. Not only do we need to observe what is going on with us, but we also need to observe whether other people are making the right decisions that are in the best interests of all. Then, we will be able to make better decisions about how to relate to one another and eventually, help transform the world.

SPIRITS AND DEMONS

Other than what we know here on Earth, do other life forms exist? Are aliens, ghosts, spirits and demons simply a product of our imagination, or our need for them to exist? Do they come from some external source or are they self-generated? Simply put, nobody knows for certain. What we do know is that with practice, the guidance of supernatural spiritual beings become available to us. This is where we find or create the angels and spirits that are ready and eager to act as mediators between ourselves and the ultimate spirit of love. This is where we protect ourselves from the negativity of ghosts and demons. We only need to practice seeking the proper help and learning to listen for it.

Spirits

Viewed mathematically, it is quite probable that we are not alone in the universe. The odds are decidedly against the fact that human beings are the only manifestations of intelligence, love and spirituality. We know that planets exist outside of our solar system as hundreds have been discovered. Although life forms other than Earth's have not been proven, there is certainly a probability that they could exist somewhere in the universe. Scientific evidence suggests that the universe we know came into being with a "Big Bang" over thirteen billion years ago. It is thought that many solar systems began forming a few billion years after and many could have developed life-supporting solar systems. Our own solar system is estimated to have formed only about 4.6 billion years ago. It is possible that many other intelligent life forms evolved and flourished many billions of years before us. This is all that science can say. The existence of supernatural life forms may not be proven scientifically but perhaps they exist in different dimensions or in different frequencies than those with which we are familiar. Their spirits may reside alongside of us but are not easily recognized in our particular physical world.

Some Astrophysicists have proposed a mathematical "Super String" theory of celestial phenomenon that postulates that there may be as many as eleven different dimensions that intersect with the three dimensions that we currently perceive as humans. Other physicists report on the mysterious and ultra-small world of quantum mechanics where phenomena occur that appear nonsensical and nobody understands. Therefore, spiritual beings, which are supernatural to our world, could coexist with us. Apparently, there is a human-like force in the universe that is willing to help. It is available through an introspection/meditation practice. Although our species evolved some 200,000 years ago, we did not start to proliferate until about 35,000 years ago. Human beings are but infants in the cosmic scope of time.

Demons

Keep in mind that this supernatural energy may also manifest itself in the form of "demons," or what is more commonly recognized as the devil. Again, they may come from an external source or they may be self-generated. Nobody knows. These evil spirits may be a product of many of the unfortunate negative energies of the universe. Or they may be a remnant from our not so distant animalistic "eat or be eaten" past. They may also be the residual energy from the "deadly sins" of pride and arrogance, gluttony and intoxication, laziness and jealousy, lying and stealing, hatred and revenge, greed and rape, and worse, terror and murder. These demons are easily recognized whenever wrong overtakes right, bad outdoes good, fear dominates love, or doubt erases trust. If you do experience any of these negative energies, use your free will to replace them with a simple practice of "light—love—one."

Saint Blase

Let me share one of the events that have brought me to believe in the power of spiritual beings. Some of my earliest childhood memories revolved around an internal conflict between the teachings of organized religion and the spirituality that was stirring inside of me. Why would I have this conflict at an age when most people accept the world-view taught to them? I have puzzled over this for many years. Perhaps it was a result of my genetic makeup, like a predisposition to skepticism, or maybe it was a result of a unique nurturing environment. Perhaps it was a remnant from lessons learned in former lifetimes. Or maybe it was a guardian angel leading me along a road less traveled. Regardless of where or how this developed, it would be well into my adult life before I was able to start finding a resolution to the conflict. For most of my life, I simply carried this discord internally as I dealt with the demands of career and family life. Although I was frequently troubled by the disparity between simple human love and pure love, I knew that the latter existed somewhere in the universe. Eventually, the psychic trauma manifested as an abnormal growth on my vocal cords, impairing my ability to speak. After two surgical procedures to remove the growth, it was returning for the third time when a friend suggested that I attend a Catholic ceremony called "The Blessing of the Throats." This ceremony invokes the power of Saint Blase, the patron saint for healing throat problems. Sure enough, the growth cleared up immediately and never returned. Without the help of this spiritual being, who could say how my health would be today.

A spiritual being may be male or female or they may be an androgynous spirit that is capable of manifesting both genders. One of the primary purposes of spiritual beings is to guide us in our ability to see the different sides of our issues and to help us find new and better solutions. They may come to us voluntarily, sensing our needs, or more often they come to us in response to our requests. They could come from an external source of power or they may even be self-generated. We may discover that they have a lot of things to say and a stream of words will come into our consciousness. Or they may come to us as simple thoughts, feelings, words or pictures. They can be helpful with our specific problems and goals and they can be helpful with managing the contrasting aspects of our dualistic nature, bringing more balance into our lives. As we grow, they may grow with us or they may come and go as our needs change over time. Remember, their impressions can be subtle and fleeting, so it would be helpful to keep a journal handy for writing down the thoughts and feelings you receive.

A spiritual being life-form could possibly be what Western culture has conventionally known as guardian angels or patron saints. In Eastern cultures they would be recognized as Divine Spirits. Perhaps they are a variation of what some have called spirit guides. Maybe they are the residual energy of deceased ancestors or renowned prophets. Or they may be the collective loving energies of millions of loving human beings coming together in the form of pure love. Regardless of who or what they are, we need to talk to them and we need to listen. They are a form of energy and intelligence that is willing and eager to assist us in our evolutionary journey through life.

It may help to use more personal names rather than the "Male-Female" or "Lord-God" invocations of Part I. I have long felt that there were numerous spiritual beings in my life that I could easily turn to for help. They can be thought of as existing in four categories: healers for the body, teachers for the mind, guides for the heart, and pure love for the soul. Over the years, I have come to know and love four personalities that have been a tremendous assistance to me. They are detailed here with the hope that you will be opened to a greater diversity in your personal journey for the spiritual beings that work for you.

Tony

Tony was a highly regarded 16th century Italian Renaissance priest. He was a leader in the Roman Catholic Church and during his lifetime he rose through the ranks to its highest echelons. Tony was a preacher of love who could have written a book like this but the church had its own agenda. To us, he is available for help with directing the behavior of the body. He is open to helping us with the moment-by-moment decision making that is required when we are dealing with the ever-present now. Because he is associated with the physical/realist aspects of life, Tony is a "healer" who gives us new perspectives on the realities we find ourselves involved with.

Howard

Howard was a 19th century English country gentleman born with a noble inheritance. He was always financially comfortable during his life so he was able to spend a lot of his time studying classic literature and world's wisdom traditions. I suspect that Howard had the philosophy of this book mapped out in his head but he appears to have suffered an untimely death. Here, he is a "teacher" who is able to help out with the intellect of the mind. He may offer new understanding into the knowledge that we already have or he may direct our inquiries along new paths, helping us to develop new innovations in the process.

Madeline

Madeline was a modern 20th century American mother and business woman. She was born into a successful household and came of age during the 1930's. She would have risen to the top of local society except that her husband was an alcoholic. Rather than becoming bitter, she developed her loving powers. Consequently, she is a "guide" for the feelings of the heart, helping to soothe its frustrations so that its loving intuitions can blossom. She offers a bridge between simple human love and Pure Love, a love so powerful that it overwhelms the negative emotions of fear and doubt.

Mary

Mary represents the purest of Pure Spirit, an unconditional mother's love that is available to comfort and protect us all. She is considered by many to be the Mother of Jesus and by some the Mother of God. She may also be one of millions of Spiritual Beings with the name of Mary, offering a bountiful love that empowers the inspirations of the soul, helping us to learn the proper beliefs that speed us along our evolutionary journeys in life. She is the Gaia (mother) that brings the building blocks of earth, air, water and fire together to create and nourish life and love for all.

If you don't have a sense of these names, substitute ones you prefer; you can change them at any time. Some possible Christian suggestions might include Saint Jude of Thaddeus for the body, Saint Anthony of Pedura for the mind, Saint Teresa of Liseaux for the heart, and Saint Catherine of Siena for the soul. Learn all you are able to about any of your favorite historical characters so that you will be able to personalize your approach to them. Then, they will be more likely to personalize their response to you. Remember, we need them more than they need us. All we need to do is ask for their assistance during the deep intensity of an introspection/meditation session. They will be more than willing to help.

BIG AND LITTLE

Life can be stressful at times and in excess, stress can interfere with the ability to use our meditation abilities effectively. Physical, mental and emotional pain is a sign that something is not right with our world. It is during these times that we need to face up to our conflicts by being truthful about them, not by shrinking away. However difficult it is to be suffering, stressful experiences present us with opportunities for learning.

As human beings, we are social animals by nature and are therefore very dependent on our relationships with others. Normally, we derive our greatest pleasures from our social relationships. Certainly, our most upsetting times come from disruptions in them. Sometimes the problem is with us. We may violate the trust of a relationship by playing harmful roles. Or sometimes it is others that are acting in ways that are disruptive to our well-being. Our worst periods are usually the result of family disruptions, the ending of friendships or the death of a loved one. In these gravest of times, our emotions may overwhelm our intellect and our beliefs may distort our reality.

Sometimes the source of our impaired functioning abilities may be unforeseen changes in business conditions. In an increasingly complex world, sometimes things simply go wrong and what we think is right turns out to be mistaken. If frustrations in the secular world are hampering your happiness, it may be an excessive desire for material things—like status symbols, cars or homes—that is creating the problem. Material things may mean anything from money to great works of art. Ownership of them may bring temporary enjoyment and they may provide us with simple pleasures through the recognition of our wealth and status. However, excessive focus on acquiring things simply for their own sake does not bring us closer to other people, and ultimately we will be left feeling empty and alone. This is a lesson that has been taught throughout eternity, from the scriptures of the world's religious traditions to films such as Orson Well's *Citizen Kane*, yet it bears learning anew in our materialistic society.

An important self-help tool is outlined below. During deeply challenging times, you may find yourself unable to concentrate on the subtle thoughts and feelings that are normally available to you through an introspection/meditation practice. In these kinds of times, it becomes necessary to digress to a more personally intensive tool that I call "Big and Little."

If you find yourself unable to engage in the following practice, I would suggest that you seek the use of an objective and sympathetic listener—whether a therapist, pastor or friend—who could guide you through a similar technique because if you are blocked from being able to find your own internal conflicts, then it will be much more difficult to grow.

This technique uses a form of cognitive behavior therapy in order to sort out the more severe internal conflicts we occasionally experience. First, combine the realistic and intellectual parts of your body and mind into an adult-like partner and assign it to the 100 billion nerve cells of your brain. Call it the adult part of you, or what we use here, "Big Me." Then combine the emotional and spiritual sides of your heart and soul into a child-like partner and call it "Little Me". Assign it to the 100 trillion connections of your mind. This Big-Little duality is also expressed in its first two words of many of the introspections used in Part I. Here, you act as both an adult-like therapist: "Big Me," and a child-like patient: "Little Me." This technique is designed to help you in communicating with the inner frustrations and wounds that remain unresolved inside of you. (You may choose to personalize these partners with your favorite names and nicknames for your Big and Little. For example, I use "Big Bob" and "Little Rob.")

Big Me

When things are going well, Big Me represents a combination of our realistic and intellectual selves. It is the part of our experience that attempts to correctly perceive reality and respond in the most appropriate and productive manner. It is the sum total of all of our physical and intellectual functions. Its basic skill-sets lie in its ability to analyze our behaviors and thoughts in the "here and now." It brings blocks of information together in order to formulate new insights and solutions.

Little Me

Little Me, on the other hand, represents a combination of our emotional and spiritual selves. It is the total of all of our feelings of compassion and respect. It is the loving and playful side of our nature that allows us to enjoy life. In an ideal world, Little Me would be a five to ten-year-old child, full of confidence, curiosity, love and joy; thrilled to be alive and able to explore all of the wonders that life has to offer. Little Me is our connection to the powers that enable us to open up to the holistic-creative Spirit of Love.

The Therapy

The therapy consists of a partnership between Big and Little. Together, they have an ability to form one of our most useful personal partnerships. This form of energy is used during those difficult times when our introspective and meditative abilities are frustrated or blocked. We start by being alone, undisturbed and relaxed, while using the deep breathing exercise. You may either close your eyes or stare off into some stationary space. Here, we want to let the conversations inside of ourselves to flow openly and freely. Let all of your frustrations, confusions and anxieties come to the surface. More often than not, the severest problems will be complicated by the disruptive emotions of Little Me. Frequently, they are made worse by the fears, mistakes and failures from long-ago. These internal fears can be easily aggravated by conflicts from daily life. Little Me then becomes a "wounded child" as its loving potential is frustrated by doubts and fears. Unfortunately, these emotional mistakes and nonverbal memories can disrupt our present-day decision-making abilities, leading to inappropriate behaviors. When this happens, we need to let Big Me take charge by using its realistic and intellectual abilities to help Little Me understand that whatever happened is past and that Big Me always stands ready to help out in the ever-present now.

Usually, it takes some deep introspective probing from Big Me to get Little Me to reveal the full extent of its problems. We may get waves of emotions that need to be broken down into the different reasons that created them. Then Big Me can analyze them and put them in their proper prospective. We may discover Little Me is carrying around a lot of negative memories that remain from former problems that were never resolved. Making progress in the real world can be difficult when these kind of nagging wounds are festering inside of us. Sometimes, these emotions can be so severe that they prevent Big Me from dealing properly with reality and using its intellectual abilities effectively. In these instances, it is the responsibility of Big Me to take control by verbalizing the problem, analyzing what went wrong, apologizing for any mistakes, and learning all it can about the grief. With practice, Little Me will eventually be able to forgive its fears and let go of them.

Other times our problems may have a more recent origin. Situations such as a serious illness, death of a loved one, divorce and/or major career challenges can happen overnight. These tragedies may be difficult to deal with and Big Me may not always understand what is happening. Big Me can be easily confused or be in denial about some aspect of reality, causing it to make poor decisions or sometimes, to do nothing at all. These are the times when the mind's logic may seem useless and vain. The frustrations of Big Me may also prevent Little Me from realizing the potential of its loving and spiritual abilities. This is where Big Me needs to let go of its problems so that Little Me can use its loving guidance and intuitive wisdom to help out. There are many problems and goals that simply cannot be solved by the logical, analytical Big Me. In this case, Little Me simply draws upon its powers of compassion and its ability to express pure love. Eventually, new insights and resolutions will follow.

After the conversations have exhausted themselves, and the thoughts and feelings have run their course, create a picture of the offending experience, situation or person and, after surrounding it with a pure white light, use the cleaning powers of pure orange and the healing powers of pure yellow to dictate that the problems float off into the universe. They will become smaller, more distant and less problematic over time. Depending upon the severity of the problem, it may take a few days or weeks of dedicated effort, but the results are vastly superior to letting the problem fester within the back of your mind or deep in your subconscious. Results may come in an instant or they may evolve more slowly over time. Sometimes you will suddenly see solutions as where before you only saw problems.

Sometimes these sessions can climax in a burst of tears. Crying is a healthy and therapeutic response that can wash away the pain of past or present problems. Sometimes these are tears of sorrow for the pain of personal relationships gone badly. Other times they are tears of dismay for all of the suffering that continues to plague our lives and so much of the world. However, they can also be tears of happiness as we discover new insight and inspirations into our personal problems and goals. We may even burst into tears of joy whenever we discover the beauty of pure love entering our lives.

Pure Love

Whenever Big and Little use the power of wanting what is best for both, they are also using the power of wanting what is best for all. By definition, this is the Spirit of Love. By using this absolute love, we learn new understanding and compassion for all of the pros and cons of life. This means Big and Little using each other in a mutually beneficial partnership to help in restructuring their thinking about the strengths and weaknesses of each other. By doing so, Big and Little learn to respect the different perspectives, opinions and values of each. Both Big and Little can think and learn their way to a better life for all. Remember, both are personal aspects of your human nature and, after all, they both belong to you.

In order to make real progress in the real world, we need to uncover new aspects of our personality and new dimensions of the unique traits of our body, mind, heart and soul. If we continue to ignore our problems or dwell on the same old negative memories and emotions, then our personal growth will be blocked.

Nobody has an ideal life. Sometimes an entire career or a trusting relationship can vanish overnight. Major illnesses may strike suddenly. Some of us come from unfortunate backgrounds of pain, abandonment and abuse. Although we may never be able to recover the lost fortunes of the past, we can still use the power of the ever-present now to forgive and to give new meaning, direction and purpose to our lives. And with Big-Little partnerships, we develop new thoughts and feelings in order to be more productive for ourselves and others. None of us are perfect, nor will we ever be; therefore, these pursuits should be a lifetime endeavor.

INSIGHTS AND REVELATIONS

How the insights and revelations of the Spirit of Pure Love may come to you during your meditation sessions is not easy to detail, as every individual will be coming to his or her unique solutions. But as a general rule, the objective is to practice partnering your innate human and higher powers together in order to liberate the highest powers of the universe and some commonality in experience has been observed:

The Four Classical Paths

- Instincts from the body are most commonly recognized as the "gut reactions," "extra sensory perceptions," and/or a "sixth sense" awareness that can be helpful in recognizing the differences between the good and bad situations of our lives. However, the body may also signal problems when we experience physical discomfort and, with prolonged problems, it may even develop into disorders and diseases. But when our instincts come to us in a rush of renewed enthusiasm, or over the longer term in the form of good health, we have confirmation that we are on the right track.

- Innovations from the mind come through new ideals or understandings of the differences between right and wrong. We can also find ourselves alerted to problems when we are confused or are unable to think clearly. These are the warning signs that something is amiss. True innovations come in the form of ideals that are for the benefit of all.

- Intuitions from the heart take the form of the positive emotions of happiness, compassion and joy. However, if your heart is filled with negative emotions, such as worry or fear, this is a warning sign of problems. Your heart's true intuitions will reinforce your understanding and distinction between the loves and fears of your life.

- Inspirations from the soul come to us through pictures, images and visions that reinforce the differences between the trusts and doubts of our lives. If we do not engage in these highest powers, we will be leaving a potential of our lives unfulfilled. But as we turn to our collective powers of love, we are connecting to a far greater source of understanding and empathy than we are capable of on our own.

Keep in mind; insights and revelations are not some psychic predictions of the future. Instead, they provide guidance about what is right and wrong with our lives. They are the spontaneous moment reactions to the directions in which we are headed. They may serve as a warning sign when we are on the wrong path, or they can provide confirmation for continuing the better choices of our lives. Be advised, however, that the insights received may not always be what you would like. Sometimes an introspection/meditation session can lead to a shocking realization that we have made a mistake or that something about our behavior is simply wrong. Humans are imperfect and there is a lot of evil in the world that can touch our lives. Sometimes the functions of our insights are to alert us when we have a serious problem in our human realm.

Sometimes, insights to a specific question may be as simple as getting a feeling of a mere yes or no. Other times, solutions come in startling revelations that strike like a thunderbolt out of the clear blue sky. Insights may come in the form of a long forgotten truth suddenly retained in a burst of what the Greeks called "anamnesis," or "the loss of forgetting." Or insights can be as complex as a series of messages that will guide your journey over a prolonged period of time. Sometimes, only pieces of solutions may appear, like parts of a puzzle, and gradually a bigger picture will emerge. They may start as a feeling or a sensation that evolves into a thought. Eventually, words, plans and actions will follow. Some examples are: a commitment to achieving good health, developing a career, strengthening personal relationships or improving your ability to express pure love. Over time, entire strategies for more complex goals and for turning ideals into reality will evolve. Sometimes, if you are already pursuing a successful long-term strategy, your insights will reward you with a sensation of renewed commitment. Using introspection along with meditation allows us to access our spiritual genius that in turn inspires the thoughts and feelings of our lives.

Insights can come at any time during a meditation session, but keep in mind that they may be very subtle and fleeting. Keep a journal handy for writing down your impressions as they come to you. While this may require interrupting the session, you can always return to the point where you left off or you can start to look for ways to implement the new insight into your daily life. Your insights will guide you to whatever is best.

Messages

Sometimes the thoughts and words that come during a meditation session may feel like someone is talking to you. It can be helpful to think of these messages coming from one of the four special sources of healers, teachers, guides and spirits of unconditional love. At other times, the insights may inform us to seek the words and wisdom of deceased prophets or the myths of prehistory. The spiritual heritage of our wisdom and oral traditions may go back for hundreds of thousands of years as the voice is the oldest form of information known to humankind.

Some sessions may suggest that we need to make change but change does not always come easily because it may not lead to immediate comfort and security. Change can also open us up to some of the painful areas in our lives that we would rather avoid. Because change often presents us with challenges, most of us do not readily embrace it. However problematic a situation may be, people are often more comfortable remaining fixed in their ways. But introspection/meditation helps us find ways to make the difficult changes more easily. Sometimes they need to be taken one small step at a time.

If your sessions are not receiving responses to your problems and goals, it may be that your mind is wandering around and not engaging the power of partnerships between introspection and meditation. If you are getting a lot of confusing messages, please use the preceding "Big and Little" section to see what you can do to be more sensitive to your problems through a greater use of self-analysis. The best advice is to renew your commitment to practicing the technique, to be patient and to persevere.

As with any skill, the more we practice, the deeper the neural networks (or pathways) become within the brain, thus increasing the effectiveness of that skill. Over time, the brain becomes more "soft-wired" (through "learned" behavior) into its use of pure love. Then new insights will come to mind at almost any time regardless if you are in a meditative session or not. If you are committed to seeking answers about who you are and how to live your life to the fullest, insights will always come with dedication, persistence and practice. Again, nobody can do this for us; we have to do it ourselves.

In an increasingly dynamic and diversified world, accessing the solutions of introspection and meditation is invaluable for stress management and self-mastery. Just as following a good nutrition and exercise program helps us maintain a healthy body and energetic mind, a regular introspection/meditation practice is essential for developing a dynamic heart and productive soul.

PART III

PERSPECTIVES

*"We have arranged a global civilization in which most crucial elements
—transportation, communications, environment (etc.)—profoundly depend
on science and technology. We have also arranged things so that almost no
one understands science and technology. This is a prescription for disaster.
Sooner of later this combustible mixture of ignorance and power
is going to blow up in our faces."*

Carl Sagan, Cosmos, 1996

Looking around the world that we live in today, I am reminded of an ancient Chinese proverb: "May you live in interesting times." And what extraordinary times it is both our blessing and our curse to live in! In the past few hundred years, humanity has witnessed such fundamental changes and growth that it is little wonder many of us are bewildered by the reality we see. It is marked in the West by fears of terrorism and economic competition. For the vast majority of Americans, the tragedy of September 11 was a rude awakening to one of the facts of the 21st century: all countries are linked and Americans may be targets for a small, murderous few. After the destruction of the World Trade Center, I asked myself, "Why are there so many people motivated by hate-based belief systems?" Nobody has an easy answer, but I do know that doubt and fear can be a primary motivation for hate.

I also know that our fates as people are not isolated from the bigger picture. If a new global worldview emerged where people truly believed that "we are but a single species sharing a single planet," we would create a global spirituality striving for more freedom and good than ever before. And if individuals could see that by simply bringing more love into their lives, they could help not just their personal future but the future of this new world, we could then create a new social order based on an all-inclusive "all." As the present trends in economics and demographics show, we will have no choice.

Part III of this book is meant to support this basic message: you can help yourself to be a more globally aware and responsible individual. This personal evolution is needed throughout our planet but it has to come to us one by one. It is as simple as people creating a greater love for themselves and thereby having more love to share with others. It is my humble effort to try and show how individual efforts to add love and goodwill is linked to the future of the new humanity we need to bring to light.

But one of the most powerful social developments that we are witnessing today, at the dawn of a new millennium, is the relentless ascent of global capitalism and the rise of numerous autonomous nations and corporations that are only interested in their own success. The developed and developing areas of the world are making ever-greater strides in the creation of wealth and power, leaving the undeveloped world even further behind. Due to the entrepreneurial spirit, along with advances in management and technology, we are seeing the emergence of individuals, corporations, institutions and governments with an awesome ability to effect power and exercise authority on an unprecedented scale. Many of these enterprises have become extremely successful in their respective niches but most have only one goal: doing whatever is best for them. Far too often, these institutions—and the individuals who run them—have little or no regard for the sustainable economics that support a greater good, and this creates one of the great tensions facing world culture today: *a truly global perspective is made impossible by the handicap of self-interest.*

Challenges for Global Citizenship

- The increasing inequity between those who have economic power and those who do not. Over three billion people in the world enjoy increasing prosperity while almost a billion live in horrific poverty.

- The widening gap between knowledge workers and those who lack education. Over three quarters of the world knows how to read and write but nearly one quarter is functionally illiterate.

- The steadfast growth of global capitalism without global governance. Workers in developed regions have growing earnings, retirement plans, and social safety nets while many non-developed regions labor under extremely poor working conditions with little or no respect for human rights.

- The continuing tensions between national and global cultures. A global culture would strive to promote economic, political, social and spiritual systems that provide equal opportunity under a rule of law. National cultures have a more provincial outlook and are more likely to rely upon regional strengths, favoritism, and religious/political faith-based belief systems.

Many modern institutions have become very good at dominating their unique niches while overwhelming their smaller competitors, thereby continuing to increase their influence and power. Some institutions, like large corporations, nation-states and governmental agencies, are often in competition with one another for global dominance. They are frequently at odds with the many human rights advocates and environmentalists that propose greater global awareness. Many of these special interest groups have become very adept at influencing politics by granting financial support to politicians and political parties. It is not unusual to find them so obsessed with their self-interests—or simply trying to better their competition—that they frequently lose sight of what they should be doing: being responsible members of the human race. And we are seeing a rising concentration of wealth and power in these institutions as they continue to grow unabated. It is not surprising that in some areas of the world, there is a growing backlash by individuals and groups that are increasingly anti-capitalism, anti-globalization, and anti-American.

Even the few institutions we have that oversee global society, such as the United Nations, World Trade Organization, the International Monetary Fund and other non-governmental organizations, are often perceived to favor the rich. The reality is that there is an ever-increasing gap between those who have wealth and power and those who do not, straining the very fabric that holds societies together. The resulting reaction can be seen in a rising tide of nationalism and sometimes, the terror tactics of the severely disenfranchised.

Although capitalism normally engenders creativity, collaboration, and inspires the growth of ideas, it does have its negative aspects if taken to excess. For instance, what inspires the negative side competition, the thinking that you have to defeat others, rather than work with them? The source that may be hindering people is the long-standing problem that many individuals—and the social groups they form—prefer to see themselves as superior to others. This is an unfortunate consequence, particularly of societies that advocate the survival of the fittest. It is also quite realistically true that most nation-states are only interested in what is right for them. With the struggle for prosperity comes the contest for domination. The resulting competition could eventually lead to dwindling resources and maybe even war.

One ancient problem is that the Western hemisphere of our globe inherited a faith in an all-powerful monotheistic God while the Eastern hemisphere believes in a variety of Deities like Brahman, Nirvana, Dao, the Divine and many others. Little wonder we continue to eye each other suspiciously. Another prehistoric problem is that many faiths rely upon religious beliefs and practices that are dominated by ancient cultural standards. Many of these religious dogmas have only limited relevance to modern societies, particularly as the modern concept of science and the "rule of law" is now firmly established. The major faith-based religious systems still in use today evolved from thousands of years of practices that were originally designed to protect clans and tribes from outsiders. It is not unusual to find that many of these "faiths" are often at odds with "others," leading to a dysfunctional "us versus them" mentality. What can be painfully lacking is the global consciousness that we but a single species sharing a single planet and that we are as dependent on others as they are dependent on us.

And what is the major impact on the life of individual people? The most tangible form of our relationship to the rest of the world is through the economic web. All of us have roles to play, and in performing work we represent the company we work for. Whether we represent Joe's Garage or the United States Congress, we still have a duty to be responsible members of society. What is needed is a continuing enthusiasm on the part of everybody to do their best within their respective roles. Then coupled together with an individual desire to work with others, we can foster the common good. We can change the thinking that wants domination; we can stop the cycle of victor and victim. The challenge is to strike the right balance between the goals of institutions as well as the goals of decent people everywhere. And I believe the notion of this unity can come to us from one source, pure love.

Over the centuries, humanity has gained tremendously with the evolution of fair and egalitarian market economies in democratic nations. It was a necessary step to take from the multitude of ancient tribal societies and the many repressive social, religious and cultural mechanisms of history. But the challenge before us now is equally important: to realize that every individual and enterprise should be aware of the needs of everyone else. Our species needs to evolve toward a world where there is one love, an absolute love that empowers everything, a love so pure it unites everyone in the respect for the intricate web of life that supports us all.

I respect that the world consists of many diverse and unique forms of economic reality, political systems, social values and cultural/spiritual beliefs. Indeed, many people are fulfilled by the customs they practice, and if these customs and beliefs are advantageous to all, so much the better. In presenting my ideas, I wish to be clear that I have no intention of contradicting the positive qualities of good people's faiths. My only wish is that the ideas presented here be *complementary* to the useful portions of people's belief systems. There is no need for an *alternative* to whatever works in the best interests of all.

As we look to grow, we may find many different teachers. There were teachers in history that we may still learn from, just as there are good teachers that are living with us today. There may even be teachers outside of the physical realm, and teachers who can only be found from going inside us. However, because we are all unique human beings—no one else can do this for us—we have to do it ourselves. We all need to discover the personal God/Divine that exists within. We need to be the best possible student seeking the best possible answers for our unique personality as well as our global responsibilities. My hope is that someday, everyone will discover this enormous power that exists inside of them through the use of their own personal introspection/meditation practice. My dream is that the tools will be as useful and powerful for you as they have been for me.

"Halfway through the journey we are living,
I found myself deep in a darkened forest,
For I had lost all trace of the straight path."

Dante Alighieri, The Inferno, 1300

RELIGION AND SPIRITUALITY

"As soon as we lose the moral basis, we cease to be religious.
There is no such thing as religion over-riding morality.
Man, for instance, cannot be untruthful, cruel or incontinent
and claim to have God on his side."

Mahatma Gandhi 1869-1948

Have you ever wondered why so some religious leaders lay claim to preaching the word of God and yet continue to advocate martyrdom, terror and murder as acceptable acts? Or how about some leaders ignoring facts while invading foreign countries under the banner of "…and may God bless us all." I certainly have wondered and I can only come up with one conclusion: religion and spirituality are vastly different.

Spirituality's goal is to open ourselves up to the power of pure love in order to find personal solutions to our innermost concerns and goals. But like any other skill or talent, some of us have more of this ability than others. Nonetheless, we all have the tools within ourselves to improve all of our skills; we only need the will and the way.

The practice of religion, on the other hand, is a social endeavor that serves the human and social sides of human nature. It is the institutionalized set of values, practices and beliefs that are based upon certain leaders, myths or ancient texts. For better or worse, religion and spirituality have become thoroughly entwined throughout history in what is commonly known as our "wisdom traditions." In order to understand how this heritage applies to contemporary times, and to our unique individual situations, we need to see how they represent similar as well as very different aspects of the human experience.

Religious and spiritual practices are humanity's attempt to solve the mysteries of life. They are faith-based and cultural endeavors that help us to see ourselves as belonging to a unified whole. They are an attempt to answer the questions that are so far unanswerable. For instance, while there is no scientific proof of the existence of a God, we know for certain that love exists and that humans are easily capable of loving that which they find lovable. Scientific evidence also tells us that the planet that supports us—and indeed all of its life—has evolved incredibly over the past four billion plus years. This writer accepts both love and evolution as facts and these facts alone are sufficient proof in most people's minds to support the existence of a God/ Divine. It does not matter if we can prove its actuality. What matters most is that if we use our personal Spirit of Love, we can accelerate the powers of love and trust in our lives.

Scholars speculate that spirituality started many millions of years ago when early hominoids were becoming aware of the life-giving powers of the sun. Archeological evidence indicates that our early ancestors developed elaborate tool-making skills and hunting and gathering techniques over two million years ago. When our current species evolved some 200,000 years ago, we certainly must have wondered about the mysteries of life, death, nature and the universe.

Along about 45,000 years ago, there was a gigantic *"first wave"* of human evolution—known in some scientific circles as the Great Leap Forward or the Mind's Big Bang—when symbolic cave paintings, personal decorations, abstract artifacts and ceremonial burials suddenly exploded in the archeological record. Slowly but surely we began to realize a greater measure of control over our environment. Spirituality was also likely an intrinsic part of the *"second wave"* of human evolution when early communities domesticated plants and animals and started the sedentary lifestyles of civilizations. These events began in earnest about 11,000 years ago in the pre-writing era. Here, many pictorial and artistic artifacts attest to an equalitarian male and female society. There are multiple artifacts found that represented both male and female deities as well as other aspects of the supernatural. The roles of nature, a personal creator, and a preserver of the world are an important part in both ancient and modern worldviews.

Unfortunately, there is no written record of our specie's first 196,000 years. Although writing was invented around 4,000 years ago, it didn't really begin to catch on until about 2,500 years ago. The ancient Greeks—particularly the Ionians—laid much of the scientific, legal, moral and philosophical groundwork for Western civilization. Between 600 and 400 BCE (Before the Common Era) these pre-Socratic philosophers provided many cultures with a starting point for this great *"third wave"* of human evolution. And now we have modern industrial and information-based societies—the *"forth wave."* The *"fifth wave"* awaits the Global Age and the universality of pure love.

What follows is a brief overview of our world's five major wisdom traditions. Then, a more in-depth perspective on the pros and cons of these theologies and how they relate to contemporary times will then be offered.

Oral Traditions

Perhaps some of our early spirituality still persists in the "oral traditions" and the rich mythologies of the Paleolithic (Stone Age) cultures that came before the modern age. Some of these traditions are still with us today. Oral traditions continue in major parts of Native American spiritual practices. Many of the Hindu mantras contain elaborate oral traditions that evolved long before recorded history. Oral traditions eventually became more institutionalized when phonetic-based alphabetical writing started to became more widespread about 1,000 years BCE. For the first time ever, people were able to record the subtle intricacies of the belief systems that had been passed down through various oral traditions, probably for some two hundred thousand years. Today, oral traditions show us the rich panorama of the diversity of abstract human values, symbolic world views and faith-based belief systems.

Judaism

Judaism had many very holy people whose lives radiated higher powers. Biblical scholars speculate that sometime between 1900 to 1700 BCE, the oral traditions of the Old Testament Bible were beginning to take shape with the myths attributed to the pre-writing patriarchs such as Abraham, Isaac and Joshua. Perhaps around 1500 BCE, Moses formalized the basic moral concepts into the Ten Commandments. These prophets were some of the first to introduce the concept of a "single God" and an "all knowing and loving God" during a time when most people commonly believed that there were numerous Gods. These were the Gods that controlled the various forces of nature, or worse, Gods that were frequently warring with each other. The God of the Old Testament Bible also pioneered the concepts that the world was basically "knowable," and that it was also "very good." This was a fundamental departure from the prevailing philosophies of the time. In Genesis 1:26, God creates man in the likeness of God and commissions him "to be the master of all life"—a concept that opened a crack in the door to the idea of a rational universe. The first major Hebrew attempt to assemble scrolls and mythology dates from the King Solomon period around 950 BCE but the Torah did not become widespread until around 450 BCE under the patronage of Ezra.

Eastern Traditions

Eastern traditions probably began evolving in the Eastern hemisphere of our globe around 35,000 years ago when modern humans started to populate much of Asia. Hinduism pioneered the meditative exercises that use the colors of the rainbow and they are practiced in much of the world today. In the 6th century BCE, after Eastern hieroglyphics evolved into writing systems, Siddhartha Gautama, the Buddha, outlined the concept of obtaining enlightenment: the means for liberating ourselves from our pure physical nature. Also in the 6th century BCE, Confucius stressed family love and virtue while Laozi taught Taoism, the sacred interrelationships between human life and the compassion of pure love.

Christianity

Today, the world is comprised of over 2 billion Christians for whom Jesus Christ is the founder. Jesus, in addition to his many acts of kindness and support for the Golden Rule—"Do unto others as you would have others do unto you."—was one of the first and most prominent advocates of the idea of pure love. "Love your enemies, do good to those who hate you . . . If anyone hits you in the cheek, offer the other also." (Luke 6, 27-29). These concepts are the basis of non-violent approaches used so successfully by Mahatma Gandhi, Dr. Martin Luther King Jr., and Nelson Mandela to protest the moral and social injustices of their times.

Islam

Mohammed's teachings in the Koran during the 7th century CE (Common Era) continues to inspire over a billion Muslims to seek a greater use of God in their lives. This Islamic movement, which began to flourish in Arabia, also traces its roots back to the Abraham of the Old Testament Bible. Mohammed, beginning around 610 CE, greatly advanced Islam with the revelations of the Koran. His beautiful inspirations produced a sweeping emotional text that joined economics, politics, society and spirituality into one comprehensive faith-based belief system. But this holy document needed to address the many social ills of the time and a rigid, fundamental interpretation of this scripture leaves little room for some of the modern notions of capitalism, female liberation and personal individualism. This may be what gives rise to the mistrust of Western ideas in some Muslim sects or conversely, Westerners' misunderstanding of Islam.

Many times our individual searches for inspiration will lead us to or through these historical spiritual geniuses. In fact, most of our behavioral, intellectual, emotional and cultural-spiritual values came from these wisdom traditions and continue to be relevant today. For instance, the four basic moral prohibitions against abuse of the four functions of the body, mind, heart and soul can be found almost universally among the world's wisdom traditions:

- Stealing: the act of physically taking something away from another (body).
- Lying: an intentionally dishonest act of the intellect (mind).
- Rape/terror: a despicable perversion of the emotion of love (heart).
- Murder: the violent termination of another's life (soul).

In addition, there are four virtues (or goals) that are also found in varying degrees. These may be familiar to some as:

- Humility: the ability to see ourselves as no more important than anybody else (body).
- Reason: the ability to be truthful and free from subjective distortions (mind).
- Integrity: the ability to consider others as significantly as we consider ourselves (heart).
- Charity: the ability to see ourselves as interrelated and dependent upon one another, belonging to a greater all (soul).

We can even trace our spiritual techniques to the four categories based on the teachings of early Christian scholars:

- Petition: asking for something from God (body).
- Meditation: listening to what God has to say (mind).
- Communion: feeling God by worshiping with others (heart).
- Contemplation: attending to God's presence (soul).

Most of the people living in the world today continue to adhere to the tenets of one of the world's major wisdom traditions. They use it as the primary basis for their moral values and their religious practices. Indeed, community and family values can be powerfully enhanced by sharing faith-based religious practices. We can still derive a great deal of comfort from practicing the rituals and ceremonies of the classic faiths because they link us to the universality of humanity.

However, one of religion's primary functions over the millennia was the passing on of the social and moral codes of a particular tribe. Frequently, "the faith" was intended to protect the group from wars, diseases and social and environmental crises—a reflection of the problems of those times. Unfortunately, many of these ancient cultural standards have survived in today's religions and frequently they are interpreted as a means to separate large portions of humanity. Catholics, Protestants, Jews, Hindus, Buddhists and Muslims have had historically troubled relationships, and many groups continue to alienate themselves from one another with an "us versus them" mentality or worse, through prejudice, terrorism and sometimes, war.

Some of today's religions have taken these ancient faiths as their exclusive "word of God." But most of these texts were written and edited by many different people over time. Furthermore, scripture has been interpreted differently over the centuries. Although the Old Testament Bible contains many passages one might attribute to God, it also contains much that can only be credited to man. Even the book of Genesis was clearly assembled by different hands as the Dead Sea Scrolls so obviously show. The many contradictions in the message of scripture suggest the distinct viewpoints of different authors. Sometimes the principle of love is deeply dishonored, such as in this quote: "God is jealous over those he loves; that is why he takes vengeance on those that hurt them. He furiously destroys their enemies and he does not easily forgive." (Nahum 1,2-3). Some ancient scriptures even portray a God that is not only unethical by modern American gender standards but sometimes they even depict behavior that is downright evil: "Now kill all the men and all the women who have had sexual intercourse. Only the little girls may live; you can keep them for yourselves." (Numbers 32,17). The acceptance of slavery and concubines and the execution of adulterers and homosexuals are other disturbing examples in the texts of Leviticus. The concepts of male dominance, religious wars, plundering and revenge are common throughout the Old Testament Bible.

Even the concept of a "chosen people" implies a racial superiority that is incompatible with most of today's moral standards. Sadly, many of these ancient concepts can provide some people with a cultural basis for their hate-based belief systems. White Supremacists, like the Ku Klux Klan and Neo-Nazis, are groups that are motivated by racial hatred and are examples of this perversion of human behavior at its worst.

To believe that all of these texts, or even only some of these texts, have the answers for the modern age limits us to their unique history and to the unique times and circumstances in which they were written. They certainly were never exposed to the global environmental challenges of the 21st century. But there are still many religions today that perform mindless repetitions of these ancient beliefs despite the absence of the original need or the circumstance that may have prompted them—religious dietary laws are but one example. It is important to recognize the times during which the scriptures arouse but many religions and faiths do not and have simply become frozen with them.

Even the New Testament Bible may have been distorted over the course of history. The bulk of the teachings of Jesus were not compiled into the Gospels of Matthew, Mark, Luke, and John until several generations after his death, creating an interpretive problem that continues today. Indeed, throughout the first four centuries of Christianity, the early church leaders launched many attacks against several different forms of theology that they deemed heretical. The Gnostic (self-knowledge) bibles discovered at Naj Hammadi, Egypt in 1945 have served to reveal the many diverse forms of spirituality that the early Christians were exploring.

Personally speaking, I suspect that one of the main lessons that Jesus was trying to teach was that we could *all* be Sons and Daughters of God. For example, imagine the view of human potential being proposed with the following quotes: "The Kingdom (of God) is inside you and it is outside you. When you know yourself, then you will be known." (Gospel of Thomas, 3) Or consider: "Whoever seeks shall find, whoever knocks *from inside*, it will open to them" (Thomas, 94). But the ill-fated historical reality was that for nearly three hundred years the early Christians were a secret cult under persecution by the Romans. It is quite likely, therefore, that early leaders of the Jesus movement would have had difficulty in teaching this liberating message of Jesus. Besides, at this time in our evolution, humanity had a long history of elitist kings and priests who kept all of the known spiritual powers to themselves, and out of the hands of the common people. Little wonder that the Gnostic's traditions and personal self-empowerment have been slow to catch on.

Today, about half of the world's religions still accept the Old Testament document as part of their cultural heritage. It continues to be the primary text for the Jewish faith. Modern day Christians embrace it as part of their legacy. The result means that the Western hemisphere of the globe inherited an all-powerful monotheistic God while the Eastern hemisphere inherited a mixture of beliefs in Brahmin, Dao, Nirvana, Divine and others.

Many individuals choose to continue to use these ancient scriptures to shape their definition of God. Although the ancient ones were certainly inspired by God, we too can be inspired by God through the use of our own higher powers and by the acceptance of the Spirit of Love that surrounds us all. From a God who is portrayed as enraged by vengeance to a God described exclusively as a "Father Almighty," any attempt to impose ancient faith and cultural standards from bygone eras upon a modern society is absurd.

What is still needed is more spirituality but most Western cultures continue to see a decline in practitioners of organized religions. Although more than ninety percent of Americans claim that they continue to believe in some form of God/Divine, it has been estimated that less than one half of Americans attend church on a regular basis. In Western Europe the estimates are far lower. Even though the United States is seeing pockets of revival of fundamental and evangelical religions, these are primarily for those individuals who are seeking directions for their lives from beliefs in fixed, dogmatic truths that are propagated by religious authorities. But other people feel a need for an inner, personal and adaptable truth discovered from within. Both belief systems are necessary. We are both private and social creatures. This is why the practice of introspection needs to be merged with the practice of meditation. The partners within were designed to bridge these gaps.

Unfortunately, too many people still see their choices as being limited to either the righteousness of organized religion or to what they can only perceive as the godless mess of secular society. The deeper underlying truths are certainly there—the moral and ethical codes for managing the four problem areas of human behavior: wealth, truth, sex and violence—but the groups can still be dominated by other ancient cultural traditions. Or groups can be swayed to worse ends yet by the will of strong leaders who may be more interested in their own agendas rather than what is in the group's best interest. The sad examples range from Jim Jones in Jonestown, Guyana to David Koresh in Waco, Texas.

Modern cultures are entirely different from ancient cultures and modern people have new concerns. The reality of our world includes an enormous amount of social change brought about because of the rapid globalization of the economy, society and the environment. More and more, people are a part of a global capitalist system that involves the free flow of capital, knowledge and philosophies. The female gender has proved to be every bit as proficient in achieving economic, political, social and spiritual goals as the male gender. People everywhere are demanding freer and more open business and legal systems. We are also exposed to an exponential growth of the Internet—bringing instant global communications, virtual cyberspace communities and paradigm shifts to business organizations. Information and capital flows have become instantaneous. They allow incredibly efficient and prosperous systems to flourish, furthering the innovations and productivity that propels a virtuous cycle of improvements and a global economic boom.

We are also witnessing a proliferation of social changes brought about by an enormous variety of technologies: computers, wireless communication, electronic commerce, personal digital assistants (PDAs) and soon, nanotechnology and microelectromechanical devices (MEMS). Biotechnology and genetic engineering are not only improving our understanding of the physical elements of life but are also rapidly learning how to manipulate it. And we will see change continue to accelerate well into the 21st century: microprocessor power continues to double every eighteen months (Moore's Law), and data communications is growing at least three times faster than computer power (Gilder's Law).

The global economy continues to be disciplined by millions of individual and institutional investors with trillions of dollars of stateless "hot money" that can instantly flee lying bureaucrats, conniving merchants, self-serving politicians and crony capitalism and thus properly seek the reward of free economies everywhere. The changes to society are enormous. This explosion of liberated markets and information technology has created a whole new set of problems and goals that ancient societies were never exposed to. Our involvement in the modern world is far more complex than anything the ancients could have imagined. And the consequences of making mistakes are far worse.

Even the paradigm of spirituality is changing. Beginning in the 1800's, Western philosophy accelerated the idea that in addition to the age-old belief that God created us—or that we have evolved *from* God—we are still in the process of evolving *toward* God by becoming more God-like, a concept that was pioneered by ancient Eastern cultures. In the 19th century, G. W. F. Hegel (1770-1831) was among many who forwarded this concept. In the 20th century, Teilhard de Chardin (1881-1955) and Paul Tillich (1886-1965), were some of the other prominent writers who also advanced the concept that we can bring more pure love into our lives.

Our spiritual growth needs to be unique to each of us. So great is our pilgrimage that the first steps in our introspection/meditation journey are devoted to energizing, cleaning, healing and growing our unique powers. Then we can begin to liberate the evolutionary powers of love, service, and the global transformations that lie within. The future will belong to those who value and nourish the well-being of the body, the creativity of the mind, the optimism of the heart, and the wisdom of the soul.

"Someday, after we have mastered . . .
the energies of love, then, for the second time
in the history of the world, we will have discovered fire."

Pierre Teilhard de Chardin, 1881-1955

FAITH AND CULTURE

"Humans in various societies are capable of empathy, kindness,
even love, and they can sometimes achieve astounding mastery
of the challenges posed by their environments. But they are also capable
of maintaining beliefs, values and social institutions that result
in senseless cruelty, needless suffering, and monumental folly
in their relations among themselves as well as with other
societies and the physical environment in which they live."

Robert B. Edgerton, UCLA, 1960

Faith and culture are similar in that they both create belief systems that societies use in their attempt to make life more cohesive and secure. The major difference between the two is that a faith-based belief system operates in the sacred or religious world where it attempts to define the values, morals, virtues and beliefs that a particular group may propagate or adhere to. On the other hand, a culture-based belief system is defined as all of the secular (non-spiritual) behaviors, thoughts, feelings and beliefs that a society may promote. For instance, today most people adhere to a "rule of law" for organizing societies, replacing the traditional "fear of God." Both systems evolved over thousands of years and they continue to operate along side each other today.

Originally, many of these faith-based and cultural belief systems were developed to answer the questions that were unanswerable, such as the mysteries of life, death, social structure and the nature of the universe. They continue to be used as a "socialization process" whereby parents, teachers, churches and, more recently, the media and "pop cultures" influence values and beliefs. They attempt to answer life's imponderables, such as "Does God really exist?" or "Why are we here"? Typically, the bulk of a belief system is passed on from one generation to the next, regardless of its positive and negative consequences.

When we inherit the customs and ethics of our faith and culture, it can be quite difficult to see those encoded ideologies objectively. Yet both have protocols and morals that, in themselves, have their own pros and cons. For instance, if a group's faith holds that human existence is one of suffering, and that the individual goal is the reward of some happier existence after death, then it is unlikely that those holding this view will have much incentive to strive for personal, intellectual or social growth in their lifetimes. The results could be ignorance and poverty. But most of us are thinking and learning beings and we have the potential to evaluate the pros and cons of any of our inherited world-views.

Variations in Faith and Culture

- Some faiths and cultures may teach that the world is a dangerous and unhealthy place and that its members need little regard for their health, as life may be brutal and short. Or they could teach an earth-based belief system that values the health of the body and the importance of good nutrition, physical fitness and wholesome life-styles.

- A faith and culture may teach people that their fate has been predetermined and that one has little or no influence over their destiny. Or, why not advocate a intellect-based system that would be intelligent and optimistic and teach that we can understand our mind and be masters of our future.

- Some faiths and cultures may view the world as a violent and dangerous place where people cannot be trusted. As an alternative, how about a love-based system that teaches that most people want to do the right thing and therefore we can fearlessly grow in our love for ourselves and others.

- Some faiths and cultures may teach that God is an angry God that seeks revenge and punishment for transgressions, and that its power is available to only a select few. Instead, why not adopt a wisdom-based belief system that teaches that God is Love, pure and simple, and that its power is readily available to all.

The choices are ours.

National and Global

It has often been said that "no man is an island" and this is becoming truer day after day. With the steadily increasing global economy, the fact that we are all dependent on one another for our very survival, comfort and prosperity is rapidly becoming evident to most people today. The result is that we are seeing the slow but steady assent of a newer global culture. But if we continue to see a contest between insatiable appetites for profits and limited of natural resources, we will be seeing an increasing probability of clashes between the dominate national cultures.

Historically, clans and kinship groups have provided social order and dominated cultures throughout most of human evolution. Other primate species, with which we share 98.5% of our genetic material, also use the structure of an extended family in order to maintain social order. It is little wonder that the many societies continue to rely upon "blue blood" kinships for leadership and this is still a significant part of the world today.

Usually, we see great love, kindness and compassion in cultures. They are often well regarded in being able to preserve traditions and for developing strong relationships. However, when cultures rely solely upon their clan or faith-based loyalties, benefits may be distributed unpredictably or unfairly. Favors may be granted based on informal allegiances and personal biases. In some of the worst belief systems, they mindlessly trap people in lives of poverty, ignorance and isolation. They may teach that their members are inherently weak and that they need a strong leader to protect them. These cultures can easily result in erratic or self-serving dictatorships. The rise of terror and hate-based belief systems is but one consequence. The challenge is for everybody to separate the negative values and beliefs from the positive ones.

Despite the long history and powerful influences of local and national cultures, a more universal global culture is continuing to emerge. We are witnessing the beginnings of a global community that adheres to the rule of law, respects representative governments, acknowledges market logic and rewards talent and hard work. We are truly at the dawn of the Global Age as over one half of the world's population is connected wirelessly or through the Internet. By the end of the second decade of this century, nearly everybody will be. This proliferation of information is empowering people everywhere. It is creating jobs, wealth and social awareness throughout the global community. In *India Unbound* (Knopf-2001) entrepreneur Gurcharan Das writes: "We have realized that our great strength is our people. Our great weakness is our government. Our great hope is the Internet."

However, this transition from a national-based belief system to global-based belief system—where we truly believe that we are as dependent on the rest of humanity as it is dependent on us—still has a way to go. Many of the problems we see today result from the conflicts between national cultures and the rising tide of global spirituality. One of the major problems has been that during the 20th century, American corporate culture came to the realization that it is in the business of serving customers and that the better it served them, the more revenue they would generate. Consequently, we have seen the rise of numerous large corporations that are interested in maximizing their profits while having little regard for the consequences to their suppliers, the environment and the rest of the global community. Many political organizations and service institutions quickly learned to follow this plan. In addition to seeing the rich getting richer and the poor falling further behind, we are seeing a continued exploitation of resources and a further degrading of our environment. What we need is more global awareness and the spirit of global citizenship.

Progressive faiths and cultures define the values and belief systems that promote and enhance human progress along the proper economic, political and social lines. More and more of us are realizing that we are as dependent on others as others are dependent on us. After all, we are but a single species sharing a single planet and this is the only home we will ever know. In the same way that people everywhere have the innate ability to know what is right for themselves, they also have the ability to be aware of what is right for others. What is essential for a more righteous global culture is the common sense convictions that health is better than sickness, knowledge is better than ignorance, prosperity is better than poverty and that wisdom is better that conceit.

Our strongest and deepest desire is to love and to be loved. The universality of love is undeniable. It is manifested in the countless acts of kindness that decent people everywhere bestow upon one another. However, many people still have difficulty in deciding between doing what is right for them and doing what is right for others; deciding between their self-serving human powers and their more charitable higher powers. But whenever we find the answers for doing what is right for all, we have found our personal Spirit of Love.

How can we as individuals affect global culture? Most of us contribute some form of input to the organizations that we deal with; even if it means deciding on what products we are going to buy and for whom we are going to work. Consumers, producers, politicians and leaders must be aware of the global consequences of their actions. German philosopher Juergen Habermas frequently lectures about how to make global capitalism work. His main points are that people need to be as concerned about others as they are about themselves. All of us must be ever mindful of the fact that we are in this together. And the easiest way to be more socially responsible is to use the introspective/meditative powers of pure love. Otherwise, sometime in the next few decades, the competition for profits and natural resources will overwhelm supply.

West and East

At any point in our journey, we may discover that sometimes we are more comfortable using only a small part of our potential. Perhaps this is because each of us has our own unique gifts and shortcomings and it is always easier to rely on using what comes easiest to us and ignore the areas that are more challenging. But it is also quite possible that our inherited culture encourages certain predispositions in individuals. Either way, it is common for us to specialize in certain patterns of thoughts and feelings. As a result, we develop tendencies toward certain behaviors and beliefs.

Although introspection and meditation practices exist to some degree in most cultures around the world, during recent centuries, Western cultures have become more dominated by the realities of the body and the intellect of the mind. Those in the West have come to be ruled by the active, logical, "thinking and doing" aspects of the brain. Thus, they have become more dependent on a style of thinking that relies more upon "verbalizations," the "talking-thinking" aspects of introspection.

In contrast, some of the Eastern cultures—perhaps because of the pressures due to limited resources and large populations—have emphasized the importance of cooperation in societies and placed greater emphasis on the love of the heart and the wisdom of the soul. Accordingly, certain aspects of Eastern culture have become more reliant upon the holistic aspects of human nature. They have developed a greater reliance upon a more passive meditation culture associated with a "listening-learning" style of meditation. Little wonder that some Eastern and Western cultures continue to have differences with defining human rights and personal responsibilities. Although Eastern cultures continue to value order, duty and stability, and Western cultures continue to value individual rights and liberties, an underlying premise of *both* cultures is the principle that every individual has the potential for awakening the perfection that exists within. Underneath our cultural inheritances, we are all essentially the same. Consequently, through the compassion of pure love, there is no reason that the philosophies of freedom, self-expression, trust and cooperation cannot spread. The economic, political, social and cultural changes will follow.

The Apostle and Kundun

Contrasting two movies released in 1997, we see a stunning example of the differences between the East and the West. An extreme example of Western culture's over-reliance on talking is Robert Duvall's movie *The Apostle*. In this movie, Mr. Duvall plays the part of a southern American preacher who is constantly quoting Bible scriptures throughout the movie while he gets involved in extramarital affairs, gets fired from his church and, in a fit of uncontrolled rage, murders his estranged wife's boyfriend. An example of Eastern culture's reliance on meditation is seen in Martin Scorsese's movie *Kundun*, which is about the fourteenth Dalai Lama, the spiritual leader of Nepal. In this movie, most of the Nepalese people were unprepared when their country was over run by Communist China in 1951. But they relentlessly believed in their quiet meditation and pacifist truths and in 1989 the Dalai Lama won the Nobel Prize for Peace. In the end of *The Apostle,* the preacher goes to jail. In the two examples cited here, where the talking and listening aspects of behavior dominate the two central characters, there was an extraordinarily different outcome. This tells us something about the differences in these approaches. Obviously, the main point throughout this book is that we all have the capabilities to do both talking and listening, to do both thinking and learning.

Some ancient faith-based societies have gone so far as to prejudice individuals into caste systems along the lines of the laborers (body), producers (mind), organizers (heart), and rulers (soul). These people were then confined to their roles for life. Fortunately, each of us has the innate competence to develop all of our abilities. Although only a very few of us can achieve the physical skills of golfing great Tiger Woods, the intellectual skills of Stephen Hawking, the loving skills of Mother Teresa, or the spiritual skills of the Dali Lama, most of us can still enjoy and improve our athleticism, intellect, loving and spirituality. Our journey is not only to capitalize on our strengths but also to overcome and improve upon our limitations so we can be the best we can possibly be.

Perspectives

"Love is the central motif of nonviolence.
Love is the force by which God binds man to Himself
and man to man. Such Love goes to the extreme;
it remains loving and forgiving even in the midst of hostility."

James M. Lawson, Jr. civil rights leader, b 1928

EVOLUTION AND CREATION

*"Nature in her unfathomable designs has mixed us
of clay and flame, of brain and mind. That the two things hang
indubitably together and determine each other's being,
but how or why, no mortal may ever know."*

William James, 1842-1910

Realizing that the human race *has* evolved from the past is important in understanding that it can *continue* to evolve in the present and future. That evolution has occurred is based on millions of facts. The sciences of archeology, anthropology, biology and cosmology (to name but a few) have been collecting them for centuries. To deny science and evolution is to deny the basic scientific method that enabled our modern era—and gives us such wonderful amenities like hot showers and clean sheets. The belief-systems of "creation," on the other hand, are based on myths that preceded the popularization of writing by thousands of years.

With evolution, there are two natural phenomena involved. First, every new generation of any complex species is not an exact reproduction of its proceeding parents. On average, our own species creates some thirty mutations in the reproduction of the DNA of every newborn baby. Some of these changes may be meaningless or harmful but some can be beneficial. Then the second phenomenon of "natural selection" takes over. The harmful mutations are less likely to reproduce but the more advantageous adaptations are more likely to be passed on to succeeding generations. In my book, this evolution certainly sounds like intelligent design.

Evolution does not occur at a pace that is evident in our daily activities. But when we consider it from a century-to-century standpoint, there is no question that we are evolving toward a more just and loving world. Recent centuries have seen the collapse of many of the monarchies and dictatorships of old. We are also seeing the acceleration of economic, political, social and cultural freedoms. Just as our societies evolve, we as individuals can also evolve. Call it learning. While we may learn at different rates and at different times, there is almost no limit to our personal evolution. Indeed, continued learning, personal growth and evolution should be our lifetime goal. Pure love wants it so.

Adaptive Radiation

For a further explanation of evolution, consider the theory of "adaptive radiation." Using the basic scientific method—i.e., the procedures that we use for understanding and verifying the way the world works—scientists conclude that our present species of Homo sapiens is the result of millions of years of adaptive radiation. This evolution is known as the adaptation that species undergo while adjusting to a diversity of previously unoccupied or newly created ecological niches. In order to understand evolution, we need to understand that the world we see around us today is not what we have *evolved* from but only what we are *related* to. That we are related is incontestable. We all share the same basic components of DNA—the four chemical nucleotides (ATGC) that are the building blocks of life. As species become more complex, they simply add or rearrange these building blocks in new combinations in their DNA molecule. This expanded DNA molecule then provides more elaborate blueprints for life's more complicated functions. Metaphorically, the evolution of life is like a giant tree: it started its roots with these four chemical molecules but then branched off into many specialized species and niches which is what surrounds us today. And as our solar system would have it, we still have billions of years to go.

Globally, we are continuing to see the evolution of societies where freedom, equality, self-determination and human rights prevail. However, this evolution never follows a straight path. My favorite metaphor is to equate the behavior of society's evolution to the long-term performance of the stock market. Inevitably stocks grow, sometimes in a spectacular fashion, because people everywhere have the wherewithal of the entrepreneurial spirit. But every now and then markets get ahead of themselves, bubbles burst and valuations decline. During these fluctuations, the stock market is dominated by the human emotions of greed and fear. Societies can also be dominated by positive and negative emotions, such as trust and doubt. Although advancement has always been the long-term result, societies can easily have many ups and downs over the short term.

We typically see a society's earliest advancement in the realm of economics. Free enterprise usually starts in the marketplaces where there is some measure of economic freedom that grants people the ability to provide goods and services that create value and wealth. The "powers that be" are normally happy to allow this business activity as it usually means they can collect more taxes (or bribes in some cases). Then, historically speaking, what follows this economic development is growth in the power of the middle classes. If freedom of speech is allowed, political power spreads to more people. If a community has a good set of social and moral values, then eventually an enlightened leadership results. Self-empowerment, rule of law, the exchange of ideas and the trust in a vision of a better life are essential for the continuation of these trends.

Generally, whenever we see a strengthening of the middle class, we also see more popular elections as people demand more honesty and responsibility from their representatives. Information on the Internet continues to grow exponentially. Information empowers people and stimulates a greater spirituality of right and wrong. It empowers people to refuse to serve in what they believe are unjust causes. Information also motivates people to participate in issues that they believe are in their best interests.

Although the first half of the 20th century was surely one of the bloodiest on record, according to the Stockholm International Peace Research Institute (www.sipri.org)—which defines wars as armed conflicts that have killed at least 1,000 people—the 1990's saw a decrease in the incidence of wars or armed aggressions to an average of thirty per year, down from an average of over fifty in the 1980's. According to their 2008 report, we were down to 17 armed conflicts worldwide. Typically, many of these conflicts are occurring between local cultures fighting over natural resources or ancient faith-based belief systems. Certainly the world would be an even better place if we all used our transformative powers to continue this downward trend of violence.

Freedom and Responsibility

In a world that is increasingly free of national conflicts, we are seeing an increasing number of people who want the freedom to take over the management and the direction of their lives. But with this freedom comes a responsibility to participate in governance, engage in debates, and vote in elections. Everyone must become involved or else we will wind up with a government that represents the rich, special interests groups and/or vocal minorities. No one should be allowed to make decisions based on what is best for themselves and their cronies. In order to make the best decisions for the common good, everyone must become aware of the collective power of goodwill for all.

Indeed, many areas of the world are thriving. Although prosperity is well established in large areas like Asia, Europe and the United States, geographic or demographic size alone does not seem to matter. Affluence can advance in any place that has developed freedom of information, binding legal codes, common goals and a sense of trust. In fact, with global monetary, legal and governmental systems rapidly emerging, many of the brightest areas are some of the smallest. Estonia, the former Soviet republic, is an example of a small republic that is making progress. Slovenia is one of the brightest spots in the Balkans. Singapore and Taiwan survived the Asian economic crises of the late 1990's far better than some of their larger neighbors. Ireland has had one of Europe's fastest growing economies for years. Finland has prospered with wireless telecommunications because they have developed a society with a uniformity of purpose. The Hague in the Netherlands has developed an internationally renowned judicial system that is based on unassailable principles of right and wrong. Malta and Botswana are other recent examples of small city-states achieving international leadership status.

Social development usually starts on a small scale where people are sharing similar resources, knowledge, values and goals. Regrettably, these steps to self-empowerment can be marred by violence when the larger regional powers refused to relinquish the regions under their dominion. But in the future, we are likely to see these trends toward freedom accelerate as more people become empowered through the Internet and by their exposure to the ideals of freedom, justice, and economic balance. And there is no need for violence in these transformations. We only need to accept the fact that in the same way that societies are comprised of unique individuals, they also consist of unique regions with diverse resources and cultures. No single region has everything. For simple matters of efficiency, every community in a global society will continue to need each other's specialties. Then, with a greater spirit of cooperation and compromise, and a better sense that we are all in this together, we can achieve greater emphasis on doing the right thing for the common good.

However, along with the development of a global consumerist society, we are also seeing a disturbing rise in secular hedonism, i.e., the practice of seeking personal pleasure as a chief goal in life. For some people, prosperity alone is not enough. But material progress without moral progress can have a detrimental effect upon spiritual progress. Although growing market economics has steadily increased the wealth in the world, the rich are getting richer but many of the poor are falling farther behind. In a world where over a billion people wake up every day and wonder where their next meal is coming from, some of the highly visible rich display outrageous spending habits. The ultra rich may continue to accumulate wealth that is far beyond anything they could ever use in a lifetime. Sometimes they continue to accumulate wealth simply for its own sake or sometimes they use it to extract political favors in order to amass even greater wealth. Many then mistakenly surround themselves with gigantic "things," (like $300 million dollar boats) thinking that their possessions enhance their personality. Regrettably, the effect of obscene greed and the incredible misappropriation of wealth and power can result in cronyism, corruption, environmental imbalances and economic stagnation.

Morality and Culture

By some measures, the evolution of popular American morality seems to be floundering. Although it continues to maintain self-correcting economic and legal systems, its moral compass appears to be struggling. For example, generations of Americans have been raised on Hollywood movies and TV productions that portray violence, hatred and revenge as acceptable elements of human behavior. In the end, the good guys usually win, but this steady diet of violence and mayhem may be one of the major factors inspiring some of our leaders and countless young men to seek the vicissitudes of war.

Other examples abound. The TV media bombards us with pictures of human behavior that exacerbates our fears. Some people are having trouble distinguishing this media violence from reality. Numerous studies have shown that there is indeed an association between brutal imagery and brutal behavior.

Our morality can also be overwhelmed by the advertising perversions of Madison Avenue. They manipulate our sexual and social desires and make us want to buy things that we may not need. The average American male can be easily swayed by the whims of the various gods of popular spectator sports. He idolizes his sports heroes and cares more about their victories and their brand of shoes than their sometimes brutish and profane behavior. The average American female can be made to feel inferior by repeated exposure to the media's obsession with super model beauty, tragically lowering her sense of self worth.

We continue to be hounded by the relentless media promotion of sensationalism and their version of truth. Most of us have become numb by the overwhelming number of sound bites and advertisements we receive. Sometimes, in order to get our attention, the media, special interest groups and even politicians will serve up frightful scenarios of potential catastrophes that may have little or no bearing on reality. It is always easy to prey upon the fearfulness of an empty soul. Little wonder that "things" can become more important to some people than relationships. Some of us turn to various political organizations, alma maters, or even street gangs for recognition and self-importance. But too often these groups have only their own self-interests at heart. Sadly, the worst aspects of the American culture are being exported to the rest of the world along with its best.

Societies have always had different moral codes for different classes, with the biggest divergences between the "haves" and the "have-nots." Historically, the upper half of society had a vested interest in maintaining the status quo and could be counted on to uphold the moral virtues of honor, loyalty and decency. But increasingly, these moral codes apply only to a shrinking percentage of the population. Generally, the lower classes have had less of a vested interest in the "old virtues." And now, as the influence of faith-based belief systems continues to diminish, an increasing portion of America is struggling with its moral bearing. In the entertainment industry, we are continuing to see a rise in immorality and contempt of virtues being popularized. In many cases, movies may depict touching human-interest stories, but they rarely present any redeeming social values. At their worst, they portray tasteless violence and butchery. Professional wrestling presents us with some of the most vulgar aspects of the human emotions of hatred and revenge. The trashiest elements of society are also showing up in some musical scores where the violation of the most basic moral prohibitions against lying, stealing, rape and murder is celebrated. The classic concepts of the American lady and gentleman are rapidly collapsing as moral codes implode.

Artists and Humanism

Artists are typically the most creative people in society, and there have been times in the past when they were able to lead us out of a social morass. One of the most striking examples to arise in Western society was Dante Alighieri (1265-1321). He wrote *The Divine Comedy* (comprised of *The Inferno, Purgatory,* and *Paradise*) in the depths of the "Dark Ages" when most of Western Europe was suffering through a thousand years of economic stagnation. In it, he laid much of the philosophical groundwork for the rise of classical Humanism: the building of a culture that revered the development of human potential. Michelangelo (1475-1564) and Leonardo da Vinci (1452-1519), to name two others, were not only great artists but through their works they stimulated humanity to see the world in many new ways, and were instrumental to the cultural transformations of the Renaissance. What followed was an explosion of economic, political, social and cultural growth that has continued into the modern age.

Today, however, many artists seem determined to pursue directions that are meaningless to anyone but themselves. Many of our musicians and film makers persist in dwelling upon our problems and seem incapable of distinguishing love from sex. Philosophers seem intent upon impressing other philosophers and as a result, they only manage to baffle the rest of us. Religious leaders seem preoccupied with preserving ancient rituals and "the faith" rather than addressing current issues. Perhaps it is time that we start listening to the spirit that exists inside of ourselves, the creative power of the artist that resides in our souls.

The evolution of the body and mind continues to outpace the evolution of the heart, and now, the emptiness of the soul is becoming increasingly noticeable.

"From out of those waves I now returned, refreshed,
Just as trees are renewed with their new foliage,
For I came back Pure and prepared to leap up to the stars."

Dante Alighieri, Purgatory 1300

FREEDOM AND GOOD

"And now, Grandfather, I ask you to bless the white man.
He needs your wisdom, your guidance. You see for so long
he has tried to destroy my people and only feels comfortable
when given power. Bless them; show them the peace we understand,
teach them humility. For I fear they will destroy themselves
and their children as they have done so with Mother Earth.
I plead, I cry, after all they are my brothers."

Sandy Kewanhaptewa, Native American leader, 1880's

Freedom is found in the actions of individuals who are taking charge of their lives while seeking new opportunities for the benefit of themselves and others. It is emerging in companies, colleges, communities and nations throughout the world. Freedom is found whenever people challenge fixed bureaucracies and old-line institutions that are only interested in self-serving interests. Breakthrough enterprises and innovations are happening wherever there is the freedom to achieve, an expanding knowledge base, passionately committed people and enlightened leadership interested in the greater good.

Freedom is clearly evident on the Internet. Here, freedom of information provides people the means to challenge bureaucratic dominance, question intellectual orthodoxy and further social networking. The result is an explosion of productivity, growth and new ideas. New enterprises are being formed daily. Personalized products are becoming reality. Ideas are originating from scientific laboratories as well as from ordinary people's homes. Continuing education is available for life-long learning. Political activism becomes free from national boundaries. Faith and cultural practices can be examined, evaluated, modified or discarded.

Freedom surely provides the best opportunity for prosperity. The annual Heritage Foundation/Wall Street Journal survey of economic freedom (www.heritage.org) has consistently found a high correlation between a country's economic and political freedom and the strength of its economy. However, according to their 2010 survey, more than half of the world's population still lives in societies that are considered "mostly un-free" with little growth, or worse yet, live in countries deemed "repressed" where there is virtually no prosperity or growth. This means that less than half of the world's populations live in nations considered "free" or "mostly free." In their words, "...freedom and prosperity are highly correlated."

Many of us work for some company or organization. Every company needs to find their proper balance between the problems and goals of their owners, employees, clients and the communities in which they operate. If our company is a responsible member of the global community, performing beneficial services for others, our job is to seek out the most important goals of our organization so we can forward those goals. We can then make the purpose of our organization the purpose of our personal introspection/meditation sessions and seek inspirations for additional ways to forward the common good. Then we will clarify our tasks and find new and innovative ways to complete them.

Capitalism is typically defined as the efficient management of resources and ideas that result in the creation of wealth and value. It can also be broken down into the four classic functions of body, mind, heart and soul. There is the *physical* capital of labor, natural resources, money and machines; the *intellectual* capital of information, knowledge, technology and ideals; the *emotional* capital of commitments, bonding, empathy and compassion, and the *cultural-spiritual* capital of instincts, innovations, intuitions and inspirations. Capitalism works best whenever the collective energy of everyone's human and higher powers bond together with their highest powers, seeking improvements for all.

Four Priorities for Capitalism

- We all need a safe and secure place for the body to work. In order to make the most efficient use of the physical capital we have, we need to feel like we are members of a team and that we will not be punished for our mistakes. Threats, manipulations and manufactured crises may have a positive short-term motivating effect but their long-term results can be hazardous to one's health. Comfort and security is our oldest and first priority.

- New knowledge and skills are important to the mind. We need to have freedom in an environment that fosters innovation and quality ideas. As the world moves forward with ever increasingly complicated problems and solutions, poorly trained workers will continue to fall further behind. Intellectual stimulation is thus our second priority.

- We need to work in an atmosphere where the heart can flourish and where we care about one another. Whenever we have a passion for customer satisfaction and for being the best we can be, it is easy to put in extra effort for extraordinary goals. Bonding with others is our third priority.

- We need to foster a climate where trust and the inspirations of the soul can flourish. We need the freedom to find our own solutions from within ourselves by listening to the subtle energies of our spiritual powers and what they say about the collective goodwill of humanity. We need to be responsive to the communities in which we operate while accepting our responsibility for the global environment. This is self-actualization and our fourth priority.

The enlightened organizations of today are attempting to bring all these concerns together. They are changing the way we work, learn, play, and lead. They are built on the new reality, not on the "old ways." They incorporate technology, not simple bricks and mortar. They are built on partnerships of people, not on individuals working alone. They are made up of networks, rather than hierarchies of control and command.

With enlightened capitalism, there is always the potential for evolutionary progress. We are nearing the end of an "old economy" that had a mechanical model of the world where machines, mass production, hierarchies of owners and workers, and the division of genders ruled. We are near the end of a system of economics that resulted in conquering, controlling and commanding. A more natural model is evolving in the "new economy" where adaptation, autonomy, unity and creativity are important. Fortunately, more and more of us live in a world where trade barriers are falling and where merchants are our best ambassadors. In our global economy, where over $65 trillion worth of goods and services were exchanged for profits in 2010, demand is increasing for advanced skills, knowledge and inspirations. There is an abundance of opportunity for all. We are at the dawn of a new age of enlightenment.

Alas, this future may arrive in repetitive booms and busts. Although the values of innovation, teamwork and creativity have been promoted for decades, many organizations continue to be run by autocrats. Numerous power centers strive to forward individual goals with little or no thought of what might be right for the common good. Governmental agencies, multinational corporations, special interest groups and political parties can be autonomous power centers that owe their success to their ability to focus on their respective domain. The result is that we have some very rich and powerful individuals and organizations concentrating on their self-interests with little regard for global consequences. The rise of capitalism has produced many enterprises that are operating with selfish human powers that are out of balance with their higher social powers. What is needed is more willingness and authority for these groups to work together for the benefit of all. As anthropologist Tu Wei-Ming wrote in the 2004 book *Culture Matters* (Harrison/Huntington, Perseus Books): "We urgently need a global perspective on the human condition that is predicated on our willingness to think in terms of the global community"—my sentiments exactly.

The global economy and environment are increasingly affecting us all, for better or worse. Maintaining its openness is one of the most important issues facing citizens, businesspeople and politicians today. We are all inextricably dependent on each other for our very survival and prosperity. But many people continue to focus on the differences in our ideologies, politics, faiths and cultures. Because of this, there are precious few universal laws and codes of conduct. What is needed is a new global-based belief system that protects environmental rights, oversees the flow of energy, and yet allows for individual self-expression. Otherwise we are going to be seeing ever-increasing conflicts between those involved in booming global economies and the world's dwindling natural resources.

As more and more of us race forward into the Global Age of the 21st century, we are also in a race to develop a new society with the proper checks and balances for these global times. Now is the time for nations to unite in a spirit of responsibility and interdependence. This new society must offer environmentally friendly policies, educated workers, and accountability for political and social stability. If we do not, we will see an increasingly imbalanced distribution of wealth and a further exploitation of people and resources. The guidance for this emerging global society needs to come from both inside and outside of each and everyone of us. The answer is simple: the Spirit of Love.

Perspectives

"Surely as a great flame follows a single spark,
Perhaps, after me, prayer shall be offered with better voices."

Dante Alighieri, Paradise, 1300

ABOUT THE AUTHOR

Robert C. Felix has researched and practiced the world's wisdom traditions for over sixty years.

In the 1950's, he first realized there was something missing in the churches of his family. Their method of teaching spirituality did not work for him nor did it seem to be working for other people in his community. Thus began his search for a better way to approach the pure love he intuited existed somewhere in the universe.

During the 1960's, while studying anthropology and psychology in college, he became educated about a huge array of human similarities. This education reinforced his feeling that the more frequently people's actions, thoughts, feelings and beliefs were in conflict within themselves, the more likely they would be in conflict with others.

By the 1970's, through a personal commitment to seeking solutions, the harmonious opposites of the universe were becoming apparent to him. However, the potentially wondrous power of this duality appeared to be woefully lacking in most people's lives.

It was in the 1980's that Felix had an epiphany and soon thereafter the spiritual powers of the color spectrum of the sun were being revealed to him. During the 1990's, he pioneered the merging of the theologies of Western introspection with Eastern meditation.

In 2000, he published the first edition of *The Partners Within*.

www..Global-Spirituality.com

Proof

Made in the USA
Charleston, SC
20 February 2011